MUSE ORIGIN OF SYMMETRY

Exclusive distributors:
Music Sales Limited
8/9 Frith Street, London W1D 3JB, England.
Music Sales Pty Limited
120 Rothschild Avenue, Rosebery, NSW 2018,
Australia.

Order No. AM971696
ISBN 0-7119-9012-3
This book © Copyright 2001 by Wise Publications.

Music arranged by Matt Cowe.
Music processed by Digital Music Art.

Printed in the United Kingdom by
Caligraving Limited, Thetford, Norfolk.

Your Guarantee of Quality:
As publishers, we strive to produce every book
to the highest commercial standards.
The music has been freshly engraved and, whilst
endeavouring to retain the original running order
of the recorded album, the book has been carefully
designed to minimise awkward page turns and to
make playing from it a real pleasure.
Particular care has been given to specifying acid-free,
neutral-sized paper made from pulps which have
not been elemental chlorine bleached.
This pulp is from farmed sustainable forests and was
produced with special regard for the environment.

Throughout, the printing and binding have
been planned to ensure a sturdy, attractive
publication which should give years of enjoyment.
If your copy fails to meet our high standards,
please inform us and we will gladly replace it.

Music Sales' complete catalogue describes
thousands of titles and is available in full colour
sections by subject, direct from Music Sales Limited.
Please state your areas of interest and send
a cheque/postal order for £1.50 for postage to:
Music Sales Limited, Newmarket Road,
Bury St. Edmunds, Suffolk IP33 3YB.

Sony Music Publishing (Japan) Inc.

www.muse-official.com
tastemedia.com
www.musicsales.com

MUSE ORIGIN OF SYMMETRY

WISE PUBLICATIONS
London / New York / Sydney / Paris / Copenhagen / Madrid / Tokyo

New Born

LYRICS & MUSIC BY MATTHEW BELLAMY

Em   B   C   G   C*   B♭dim   Baug add¹¹   B*
7 fr.   7 fr.   8 fr.   7 fr.

E⁵   Em*   A⁵   D   G⁵   C**   Baug add¹¹*
7 fr.   7 fr.   9 fr.   10 fr.   7 fr.   2 fr.

♩=147

All gtrs. ⑥ = D

Intro

Em   B (E bass)

1° Elec. Piano
2° Elec. & Acous. Piano

2° Bass Synth w/fig. 1

Em   B (E bass)   Em

C   G (D bass)   B (D♯ bass)

l.h. cont. sim.

Verse

Em   B (E bass)

Gtr. 3 (elec.)
1° tacet
3° (𝄋) tacet until marked   *etc.*   *cont. sim.*

1. 3. (𝄋) Link   it   to   the   world,
2. Hope - less   time   to   roam,   the

Fig. 1...
Bass Gtr.

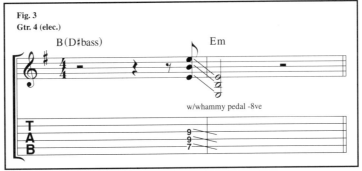

10

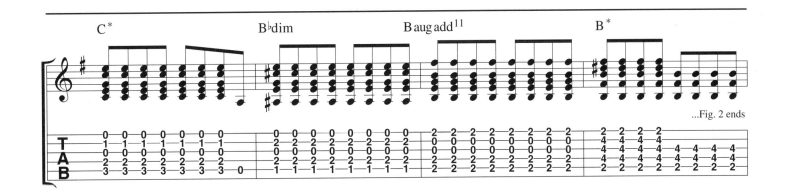

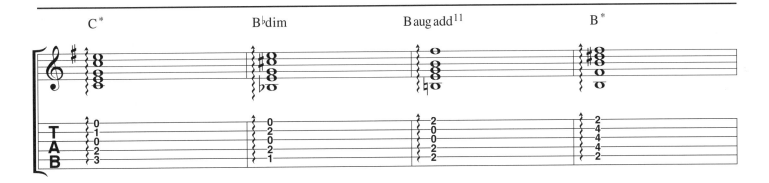

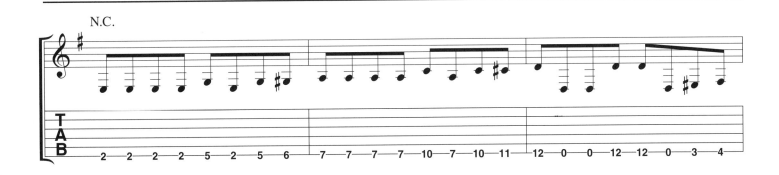

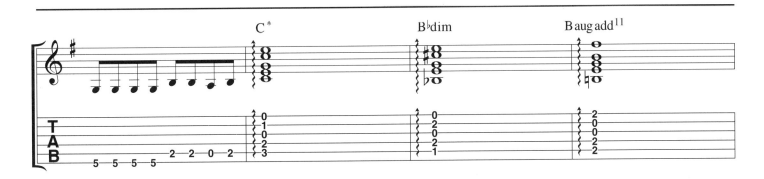

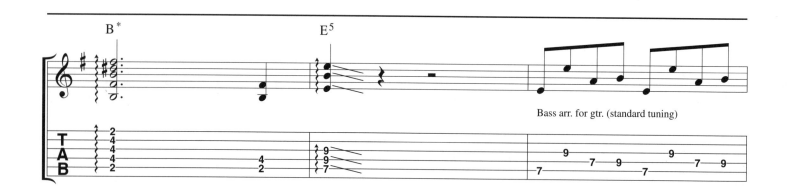

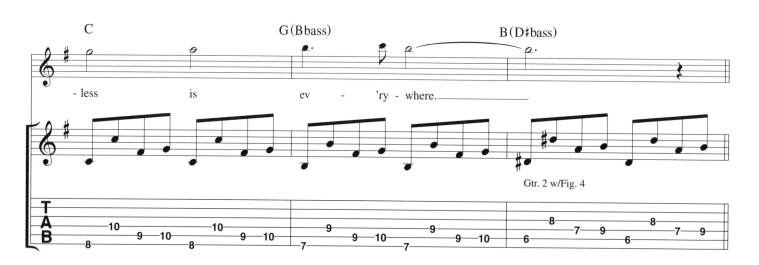

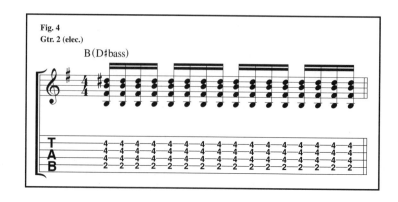

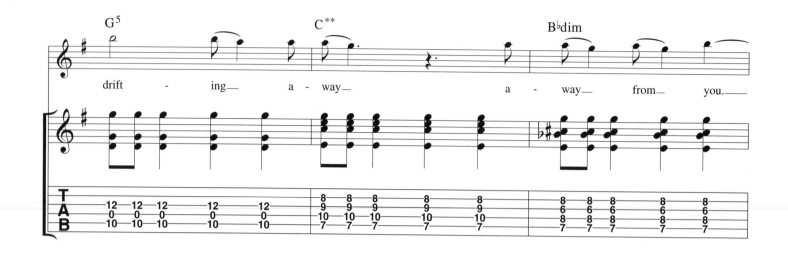

G⁵ ... C** ... B♭dim

drift - ing— a - way—   a - way— from— you.—

To Coda ⊕

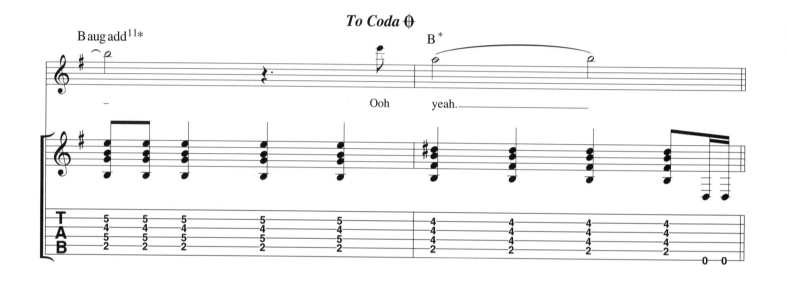

B aug add¹¹* ... B*

Ooh   yeah.—

N.C.

Gtr. 2

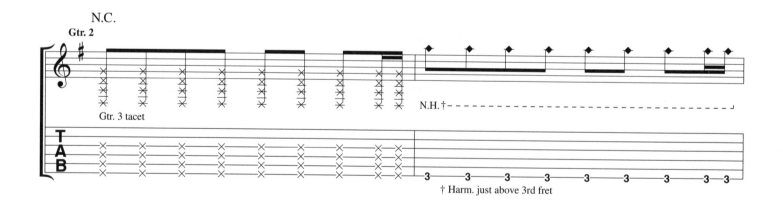

Gtr. 3 tacet

N.H. † - ⌐

† Harm. just above 3rd fret

8va -

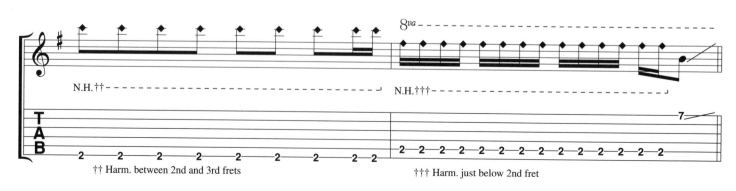

N.H. †† - ⌐   N.H. ††† -

†† Harm. between 2nd and 3rd frets   ††† Harm. just below 2nd fret

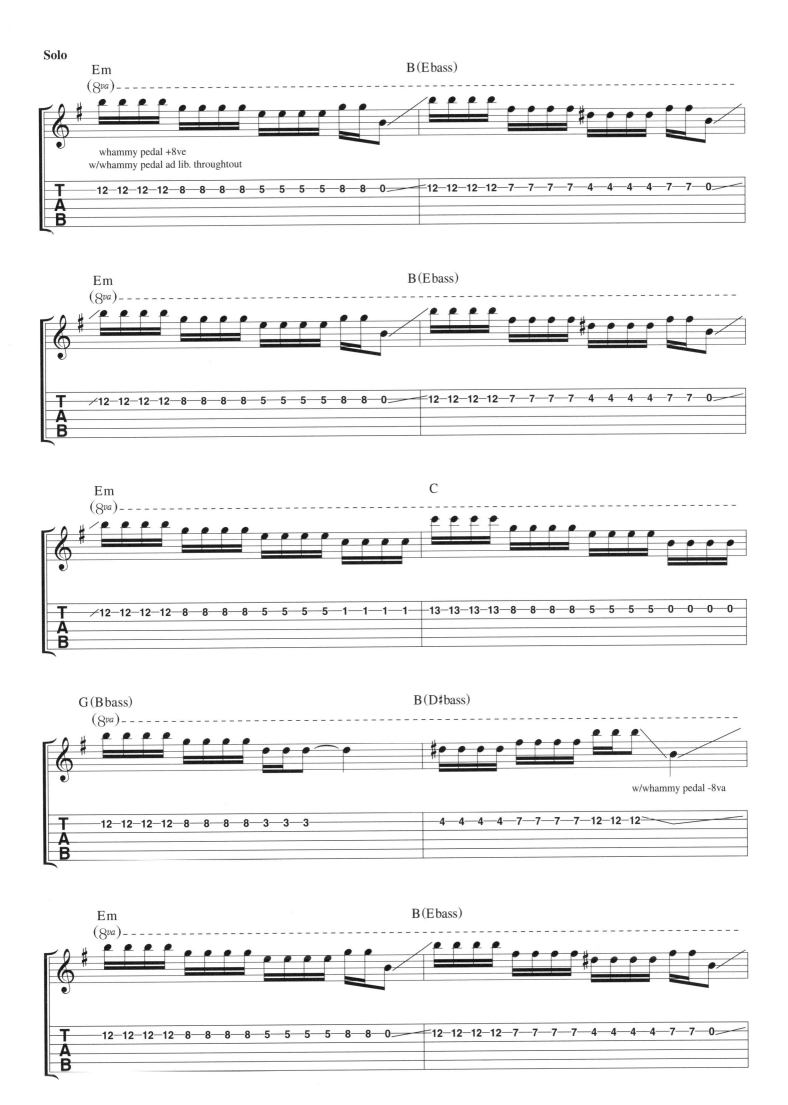

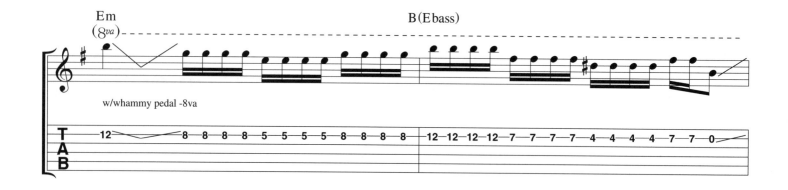

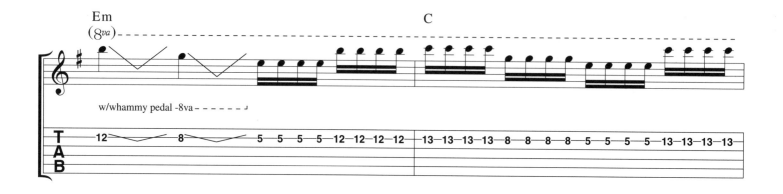

D. %. al Coda
Take 2º

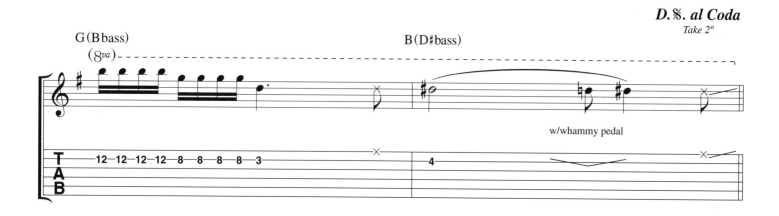

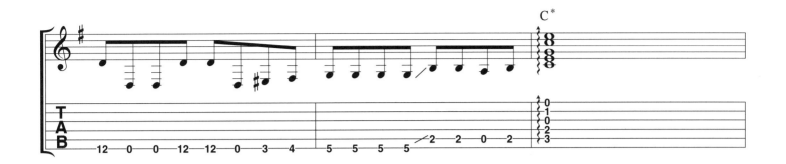

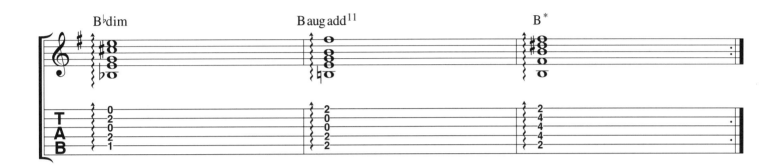

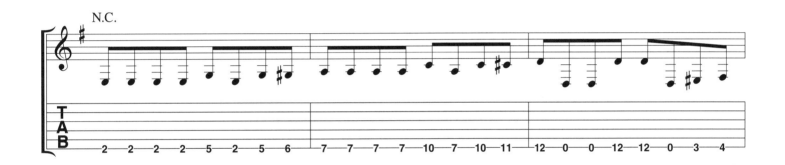

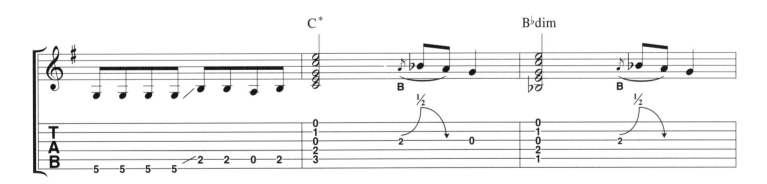

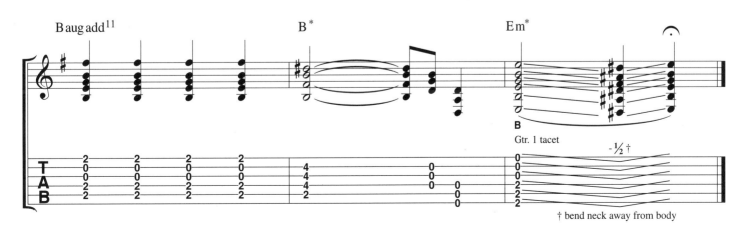

† bend neck away from body

Bliss

LYRICS & MUSIC BY MATTHEW BELLAMY

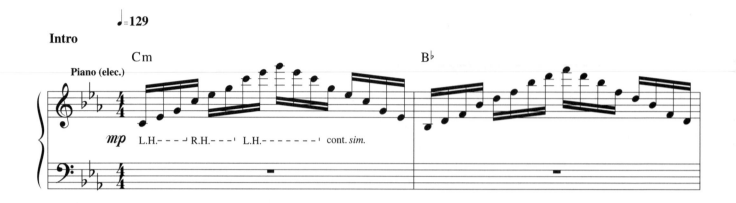

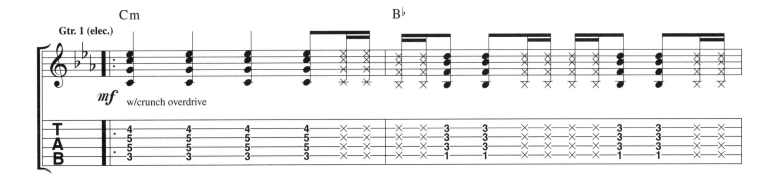

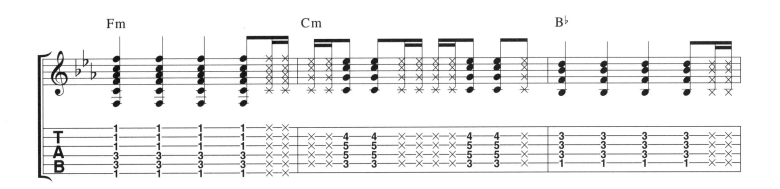

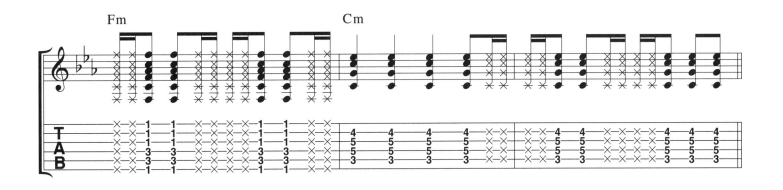

Verse

1. Ev - 'ry - thing a - bout you is_____ how
2. Ev - 'ry - thing a - bout you pains_____ my

Fuzz bass arr. for gtr.

Cm

for less.
above.

§

Chorus

C

Am

C/G

Give me

Gtr. 1

Piano (elec.) w/intro arpeggios

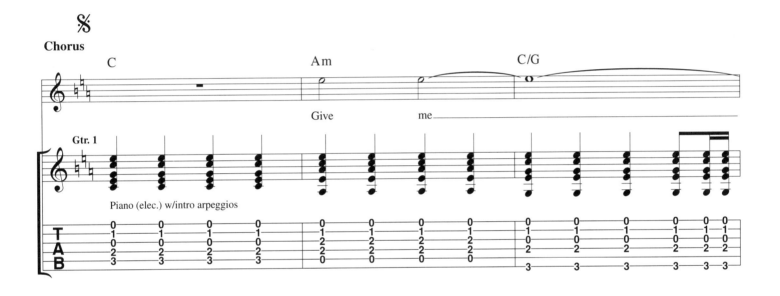

C

Am

— all the peace and joy in your

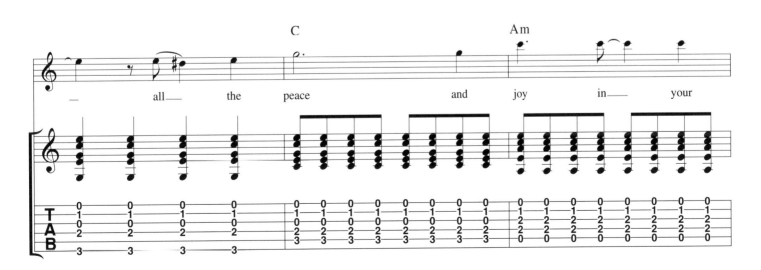

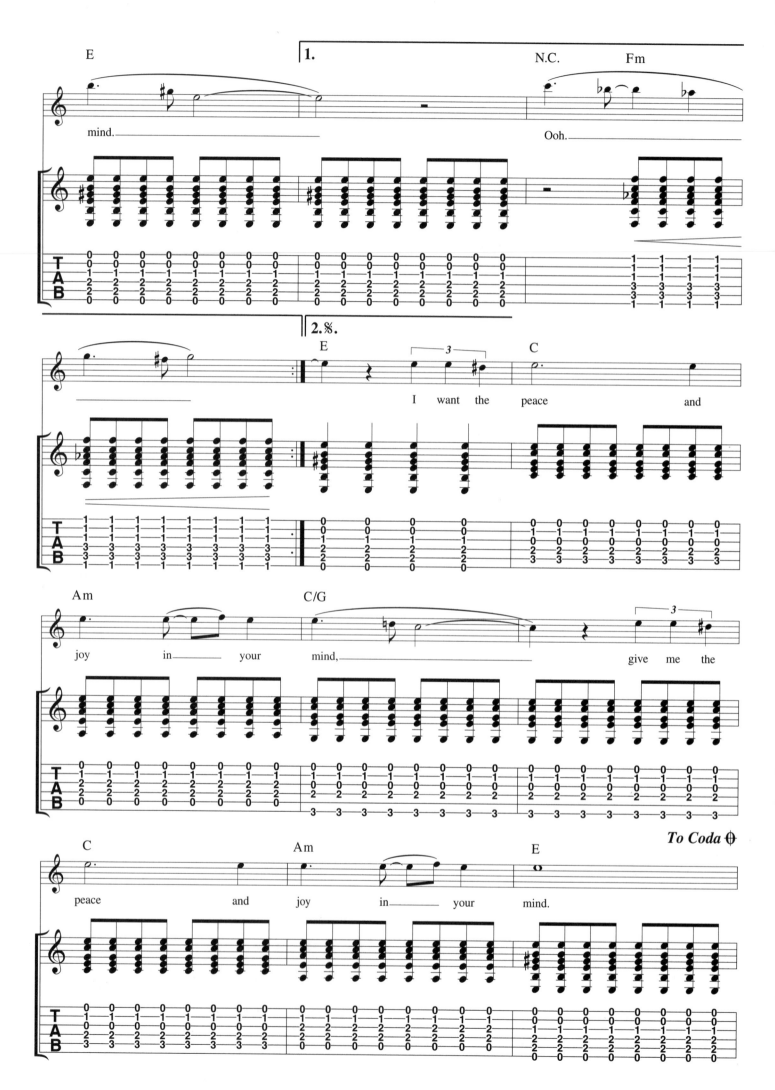

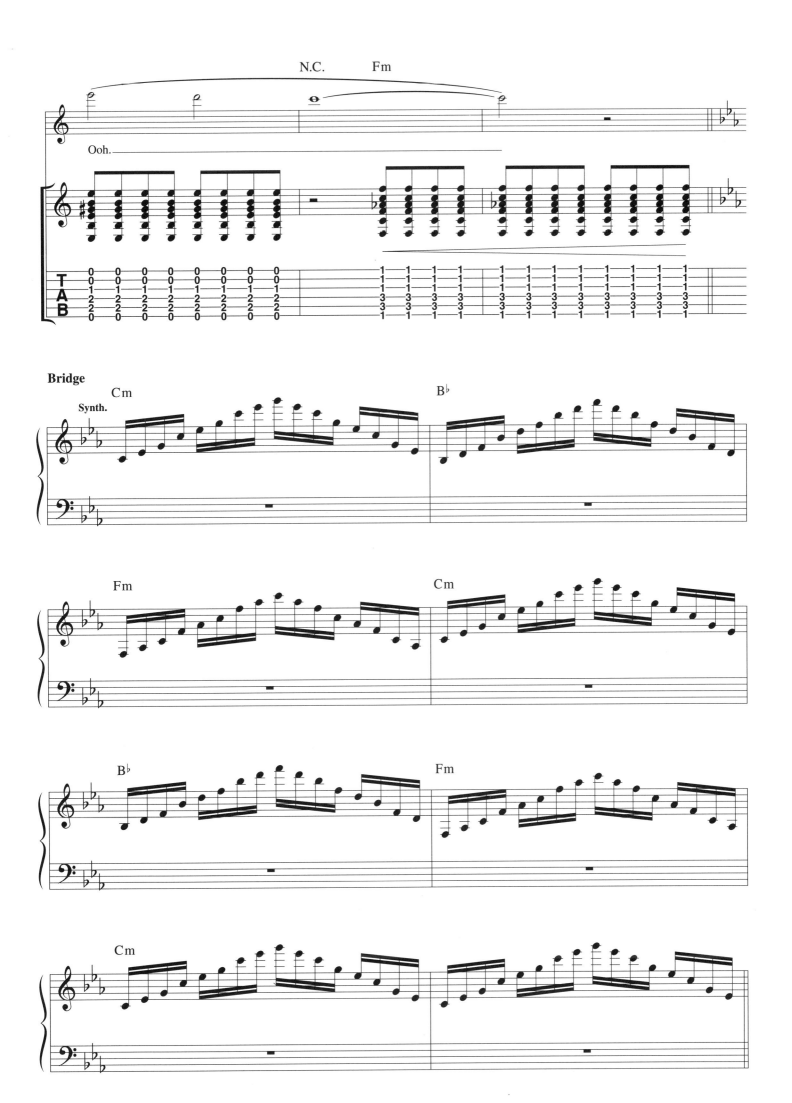

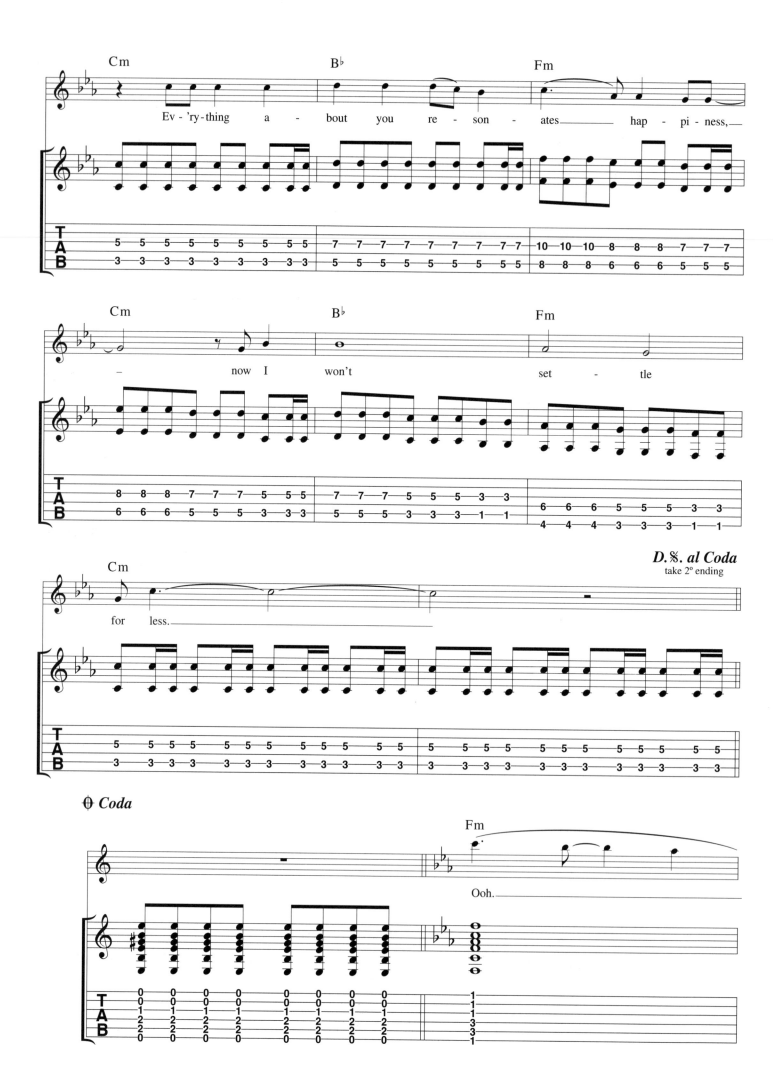

Piano (elec.)

p

w/echo

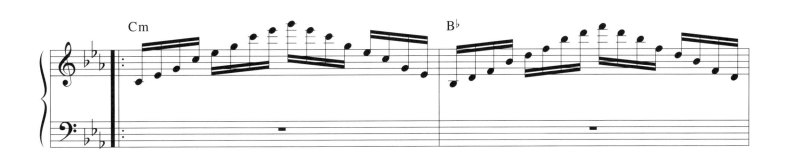

Cm   B♭

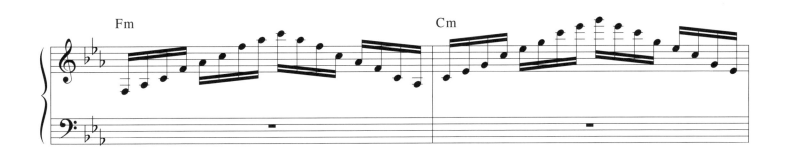

Fm   Cm

B♭   Fm

Repeat to fade

Cm

Space Dementia

LYRICS & MUSIC BY MATTHEW BELLAMY

♩ = **62** *Rubato*

Intro

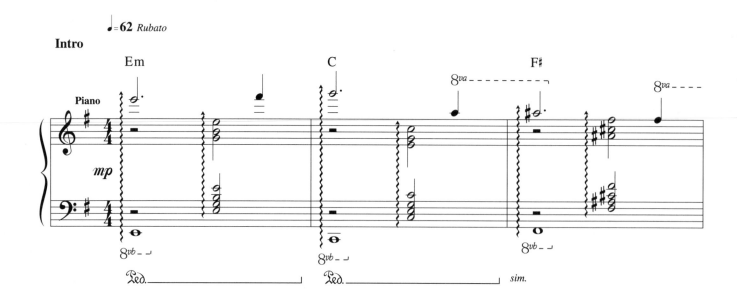

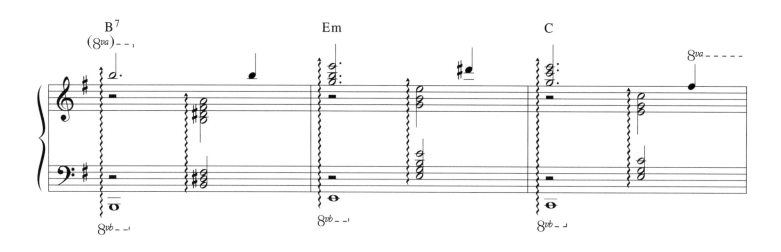

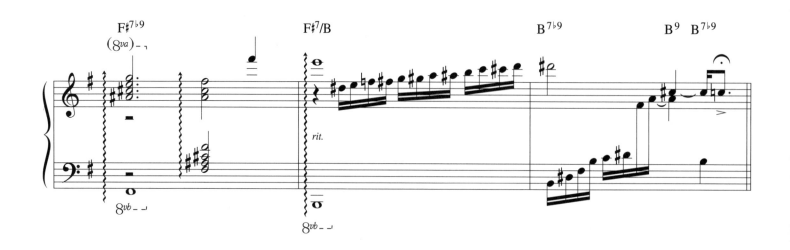

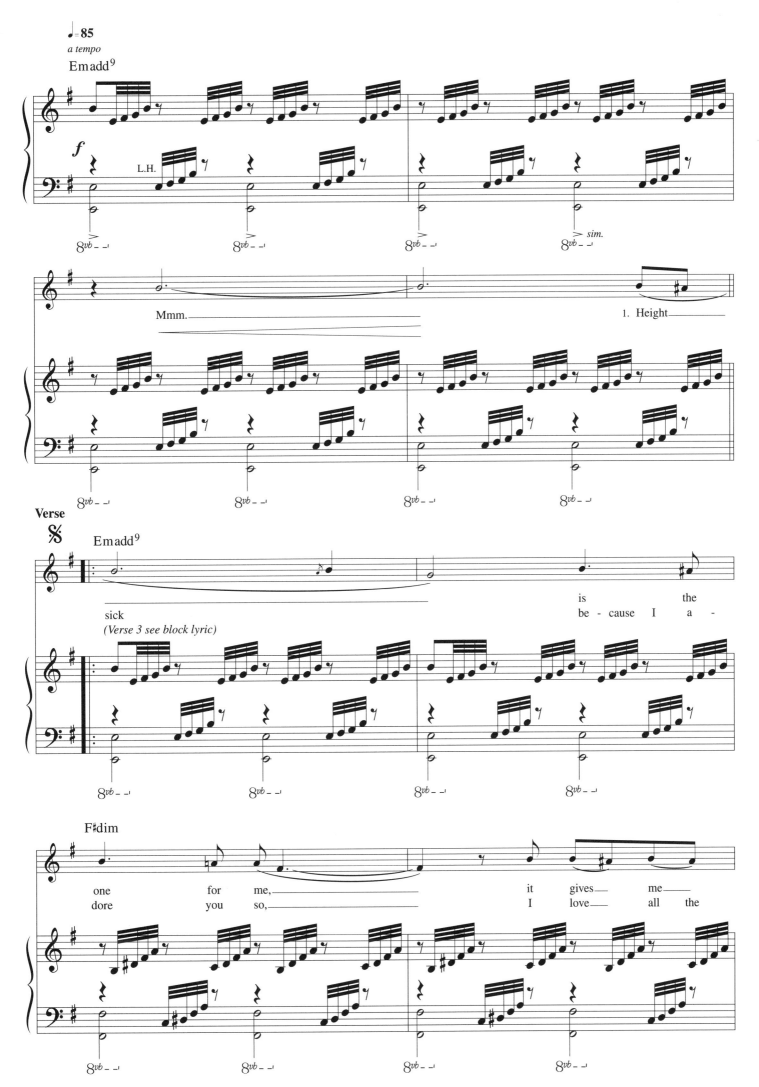

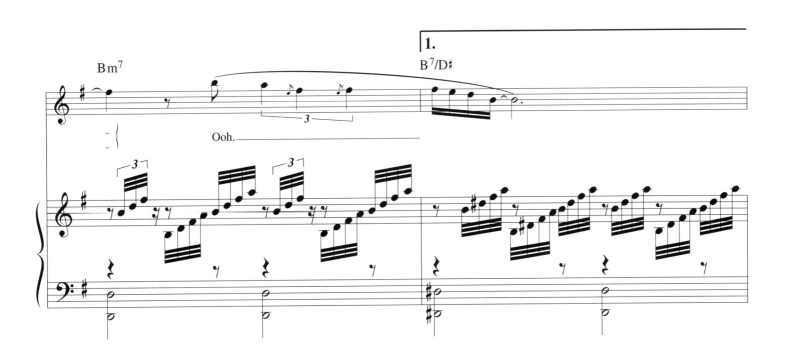

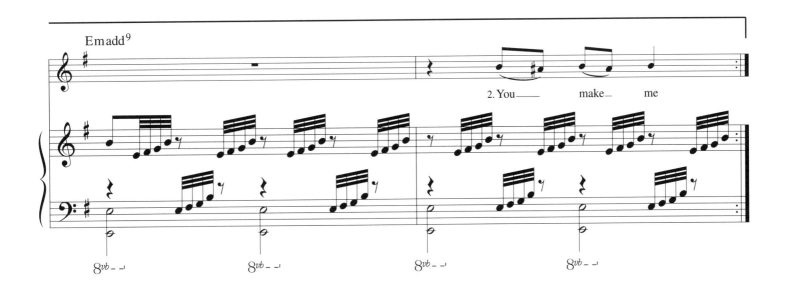

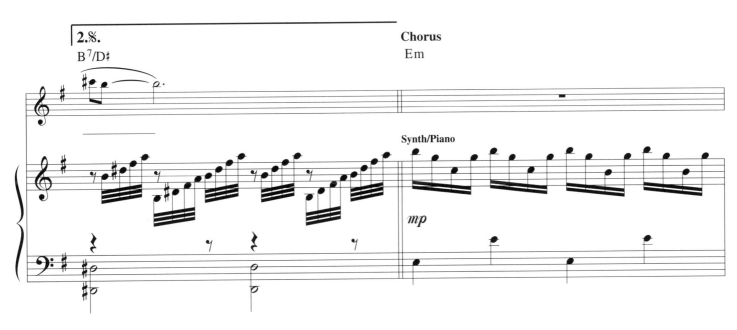

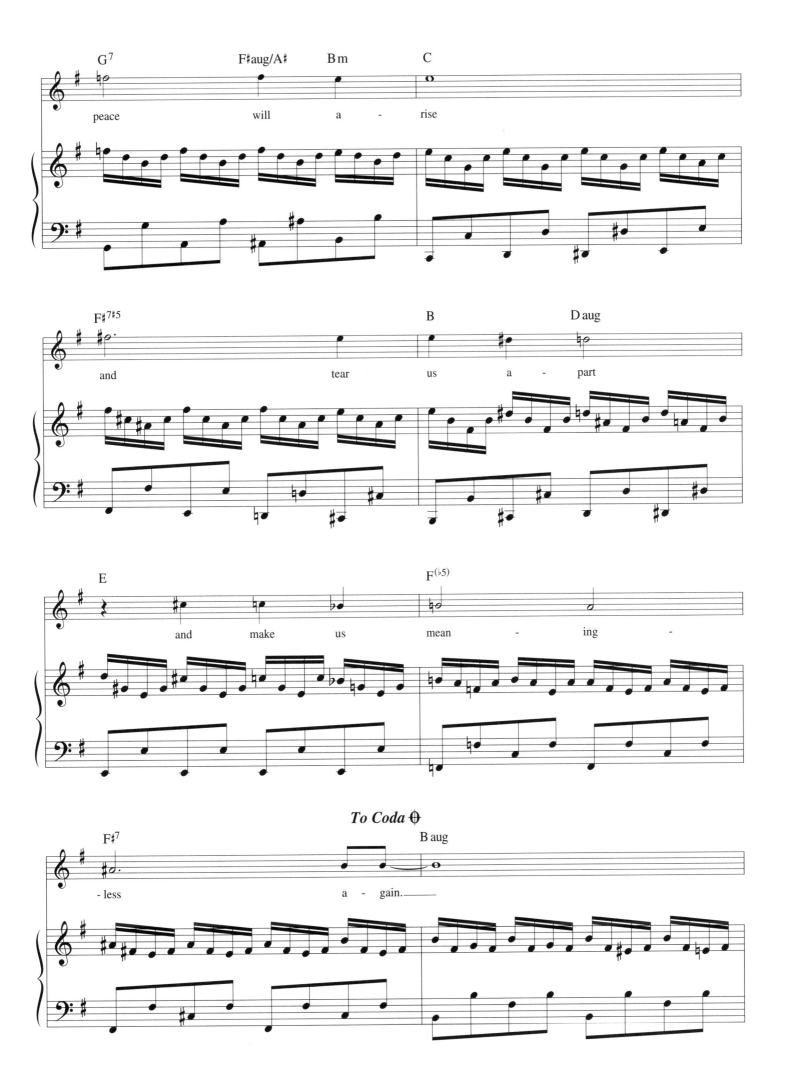

To Coda ⊕

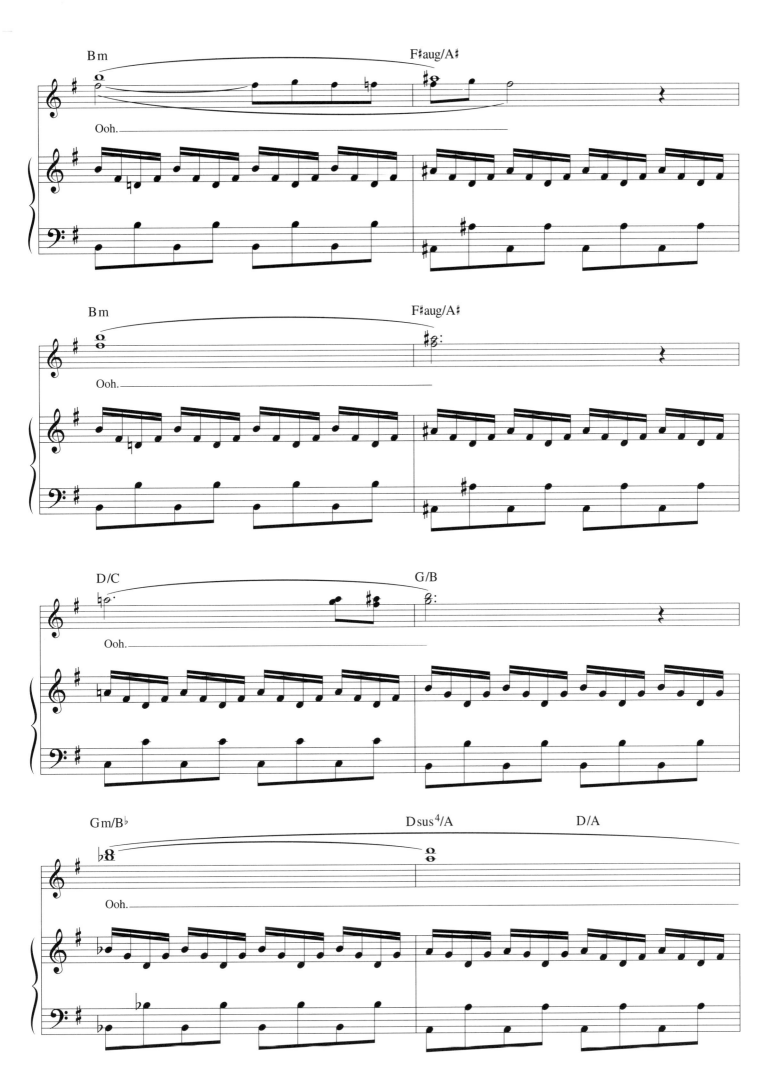

Verse 3:
You make us wanna die
I'd cut your name in my heart
We'll destroy this world for you
I know you want me to
Feel your pain.

Hyper Music

LYRICS & MUSIC BY MATTHEW BELLAMY

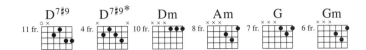

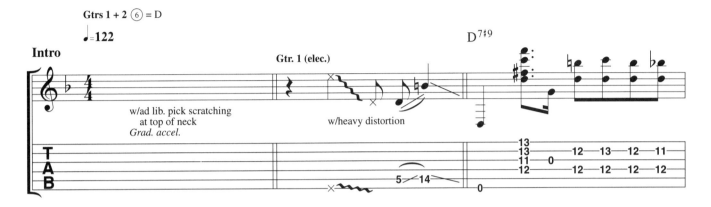

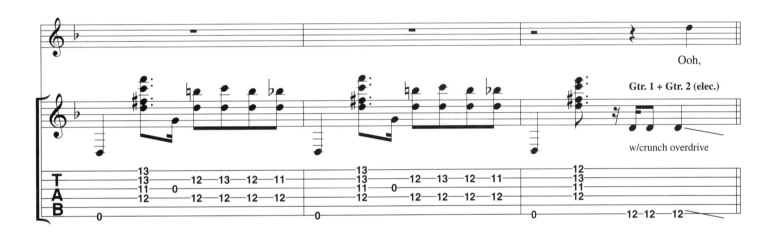

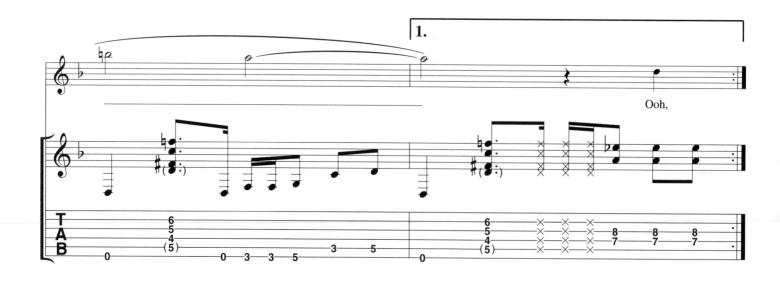

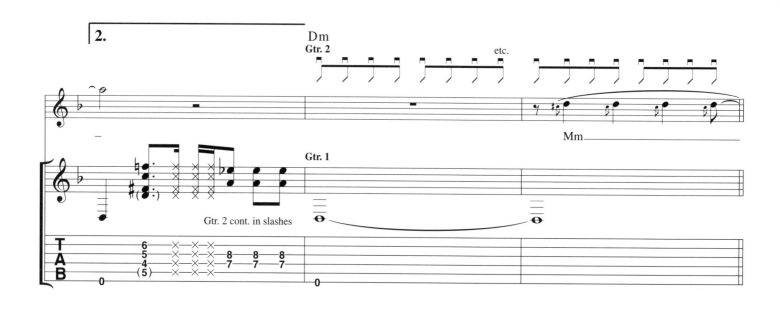

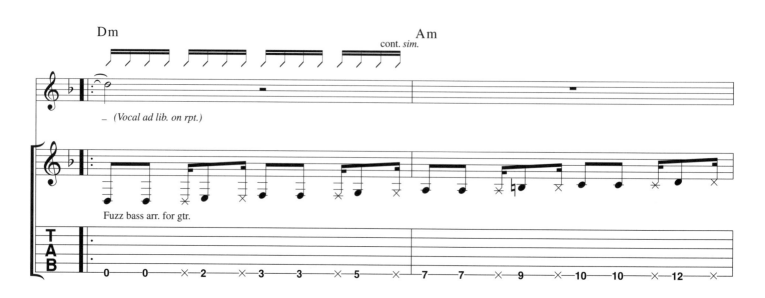

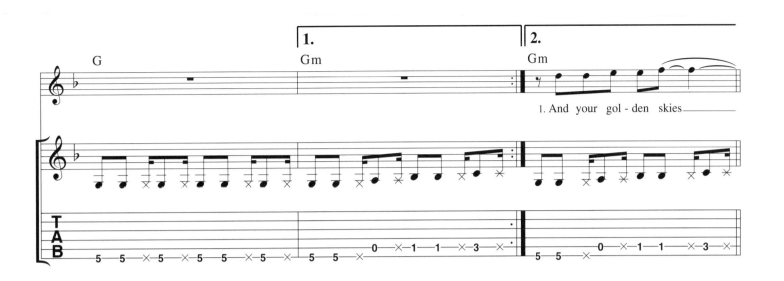

Verse

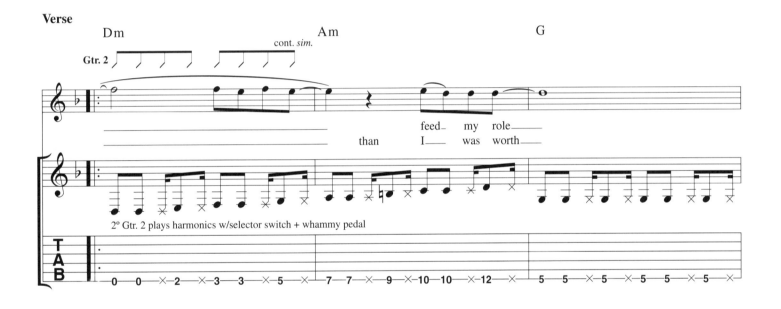

2° Gtr. 2 plays harmonics w/selector switch + whammy pedal

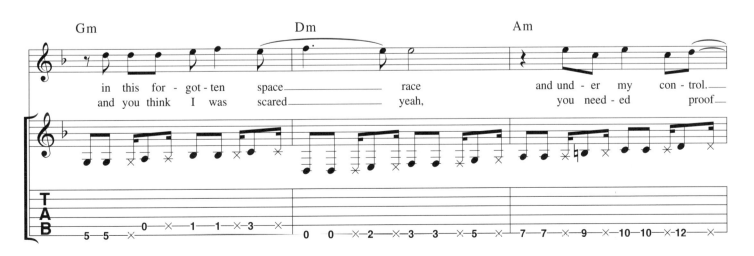

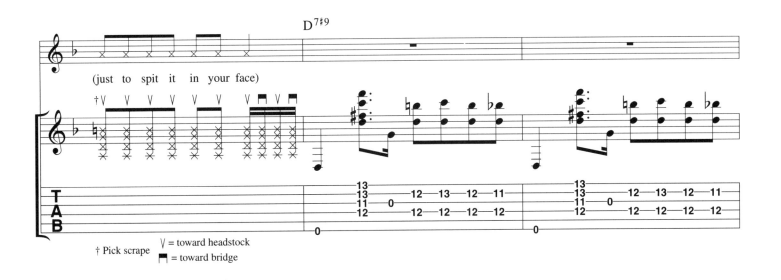

(just to spit it in your face)

† Pick scrape   V = toward headstock
                ⊓ = toward bridge

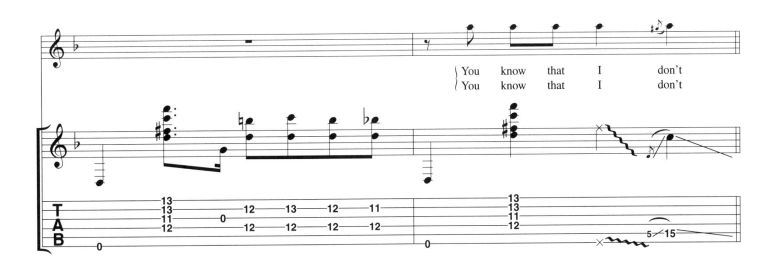

You know that I   don't
You know that I   don't

Chorus

want you,
love you,   and I   nev - er did.

Gtrs 1 + 2

I don't want you, and I nev-er will

1.

Dm

Gtr. 2

Gtr. 1

Gtr. 2 cont. in slashes

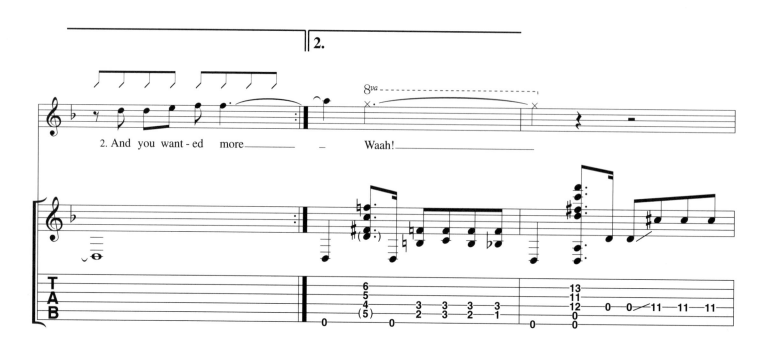

2.

2. And you want-ed more_____ Waah!_____

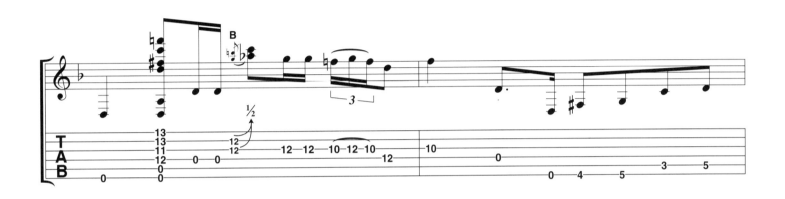

D^{7♯9}*

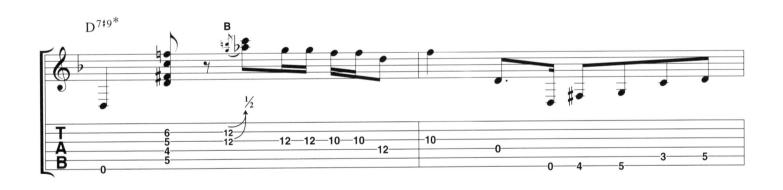

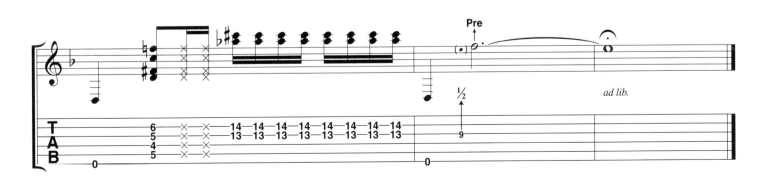

Citizen Erased

LYRICS & MUSIC BY MATTHEW BELLAMY

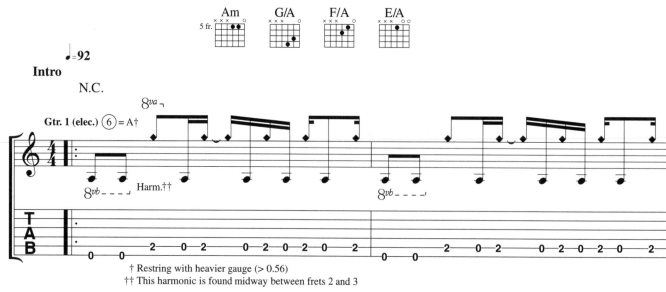

† Restring with heavier gauge (> 0.56)
†† This harmonic is found midway between frets 2 and 3

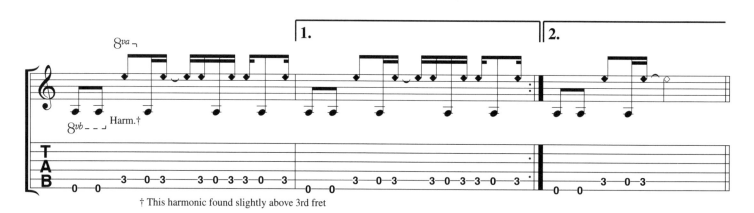

† This harmonic found slightly above 3rd fret

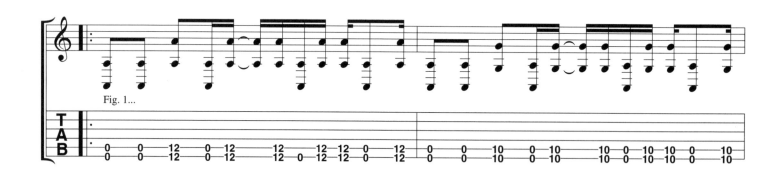

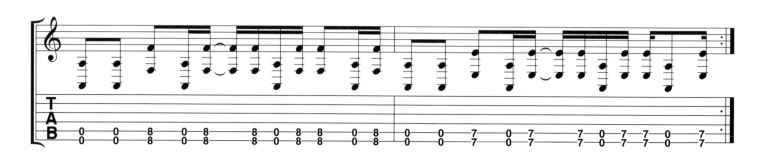

Verse

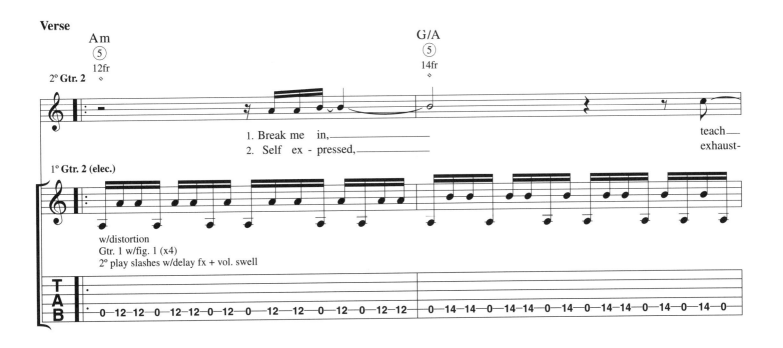

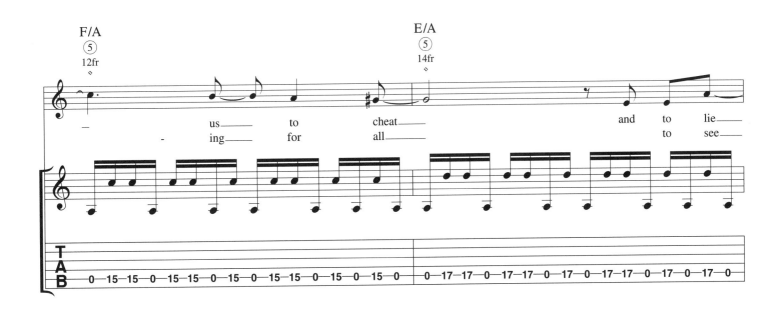

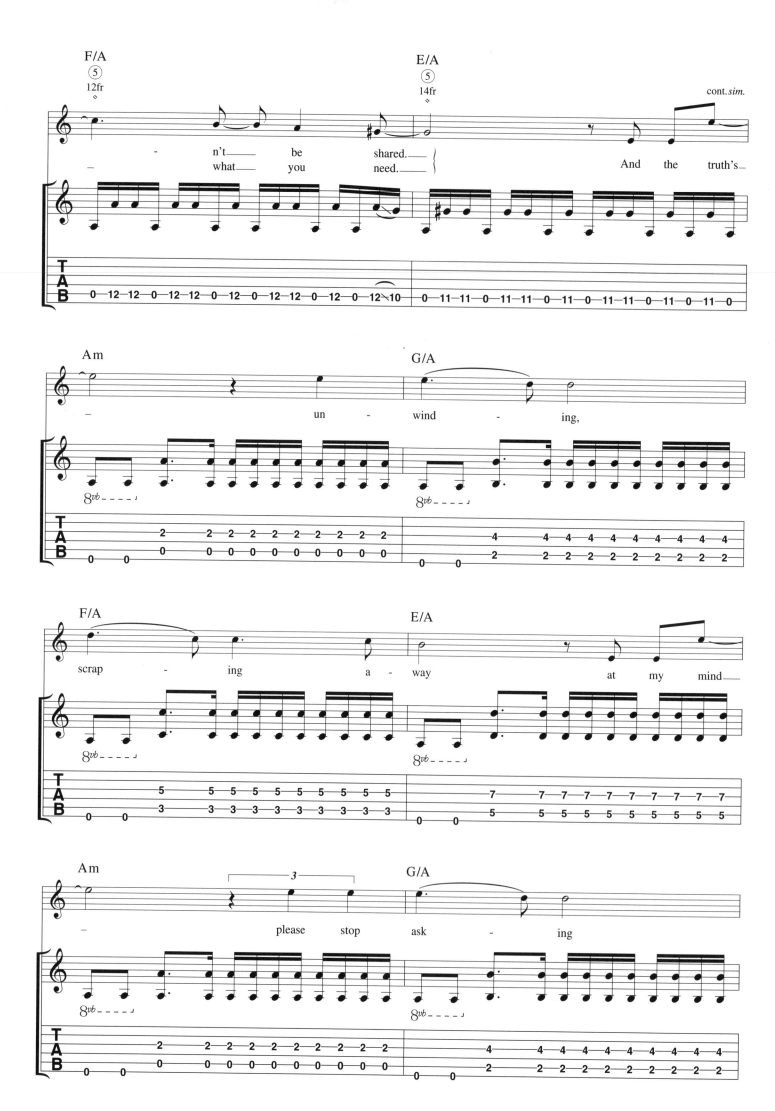

me_____ to des - cribe._____

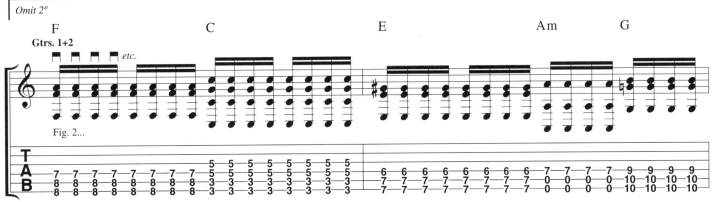

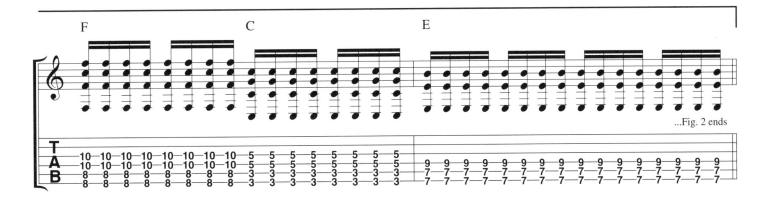

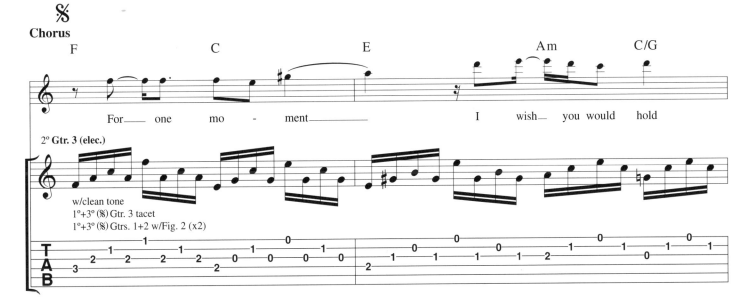

For___ one mo - ment_____ I wish_ you would hold

your stage   with no feel - ings   at all._____

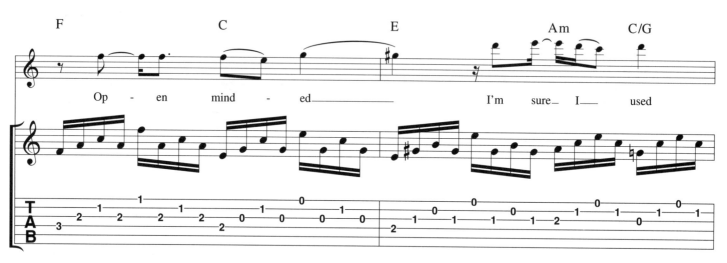

Op - en mind - ed_____   I'm sure_ I___ used

To Coda ✛ | **1.**

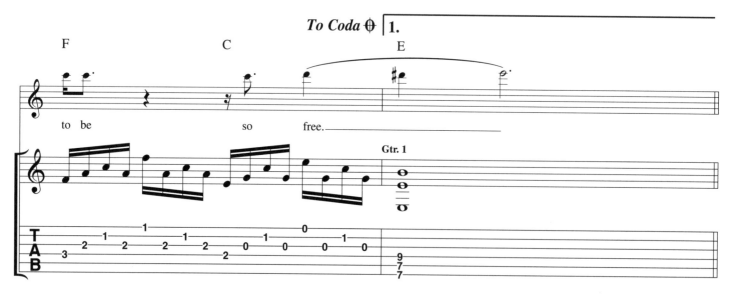

to be   so   free._____

Gtr. 1

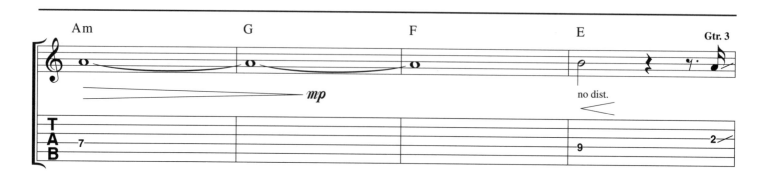

Gtr. 3

mp

no dist.

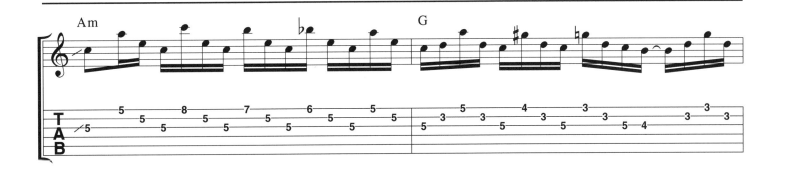

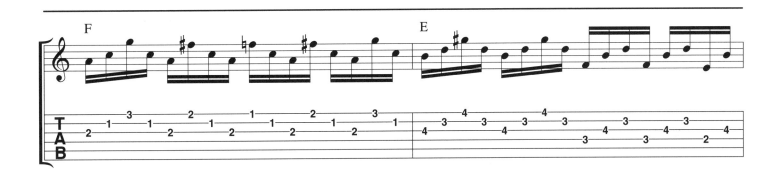

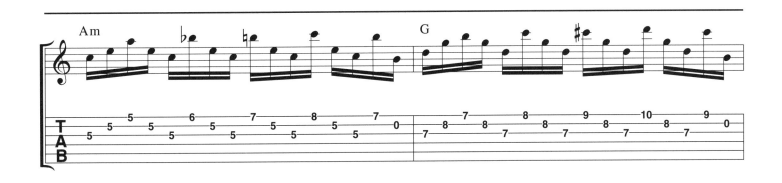

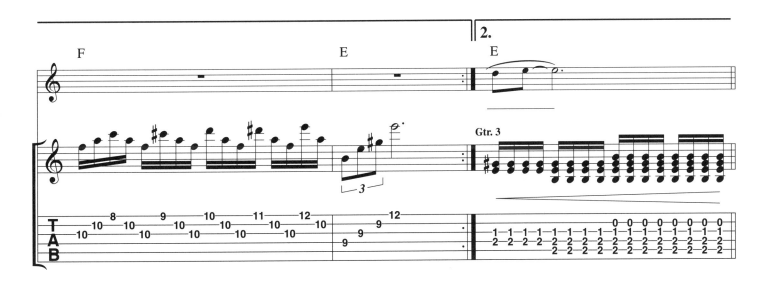

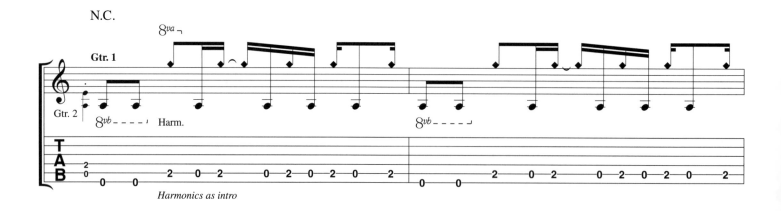

Harmonics as intro

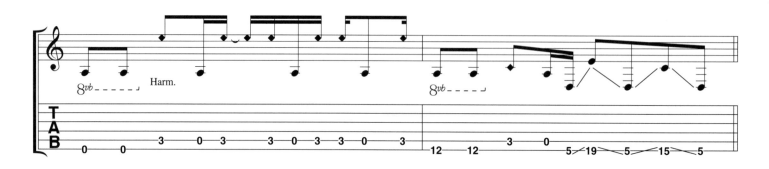

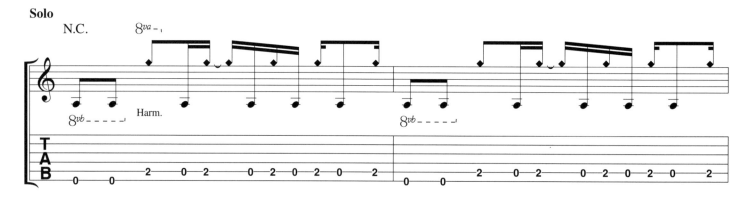

Solo

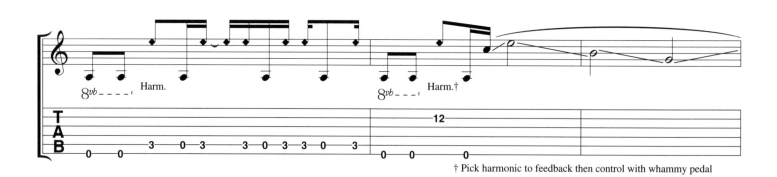

† Pick harmonic to feedback then control with whammy pedal

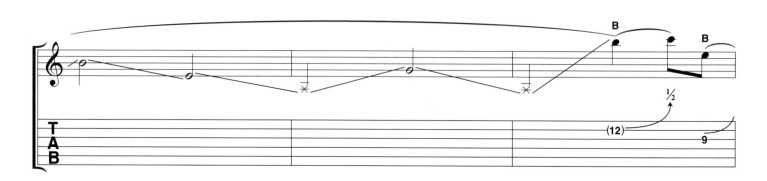

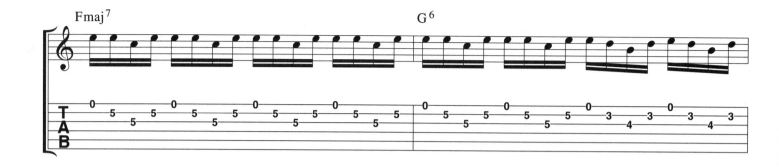

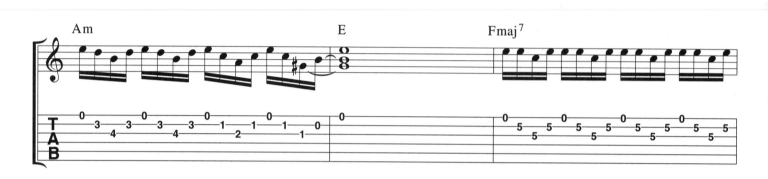

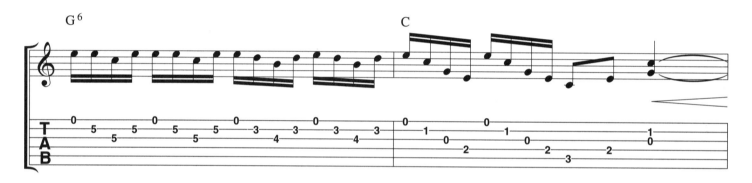

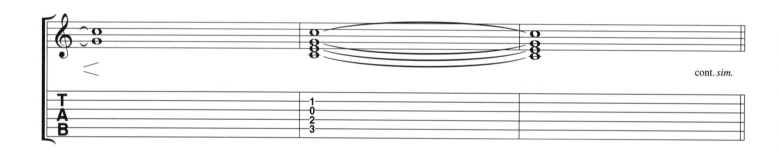

(2°) Wash— me a - way,_____ clean— your— bo - dy of me,_____

Plug In Baby

LYRICS & MUSIC BY MATTHEW BELLAMY

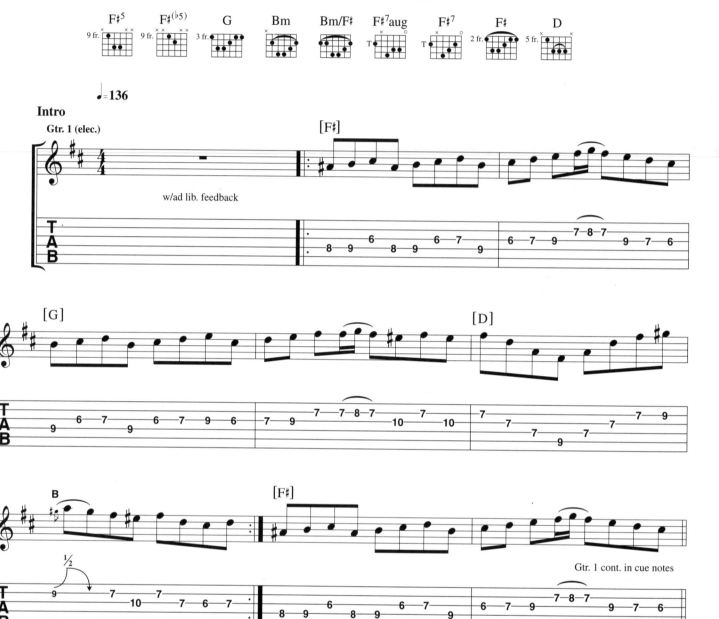

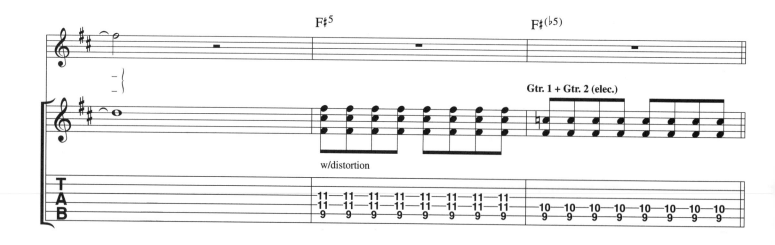

Chorus

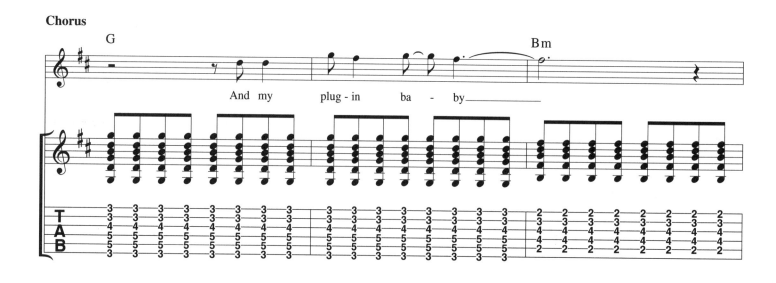

And my plug - in ba - by____

cru - ci - fies__ my en - em - ies. When I'm tired of giv - ing.____

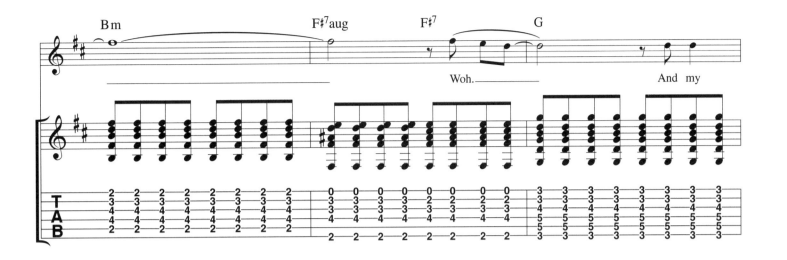

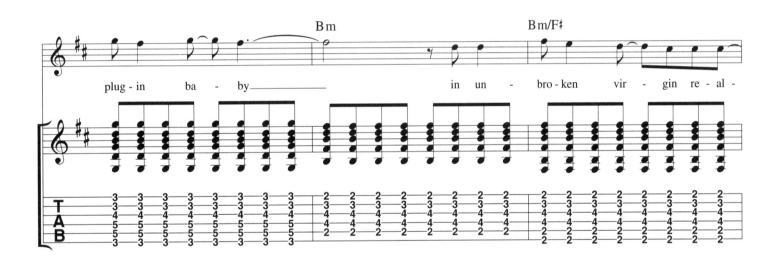

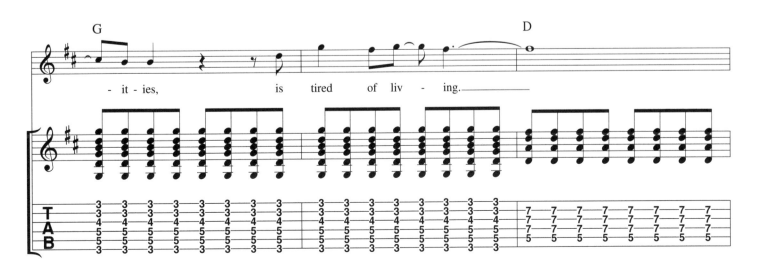

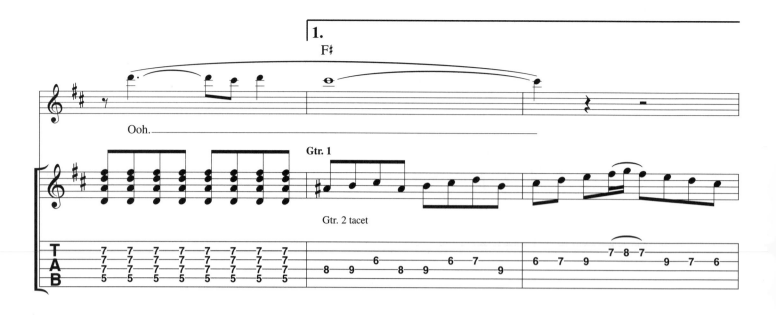

Ooh.

And I've seen____ your____ lov - ing,____

mine is____ gone,____

and I've been____ in____ trou - ble.

Woo.____ Ahh.____

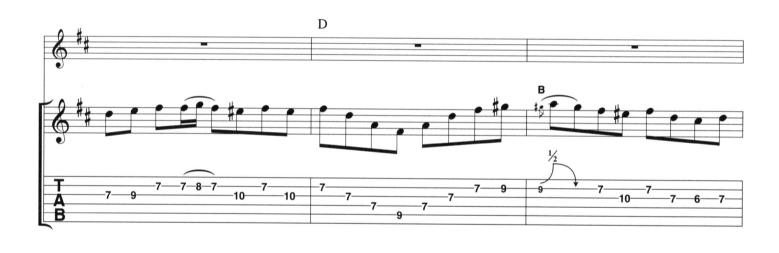

Micro Cuts

LYRICS & MUSIC BY MATTHEW BELLAMY

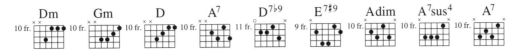

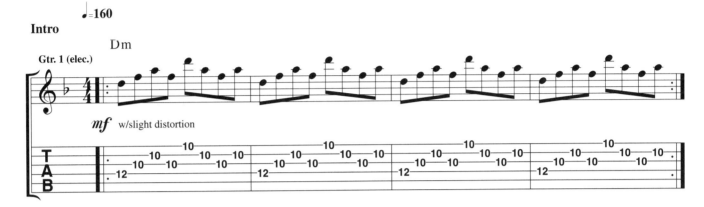

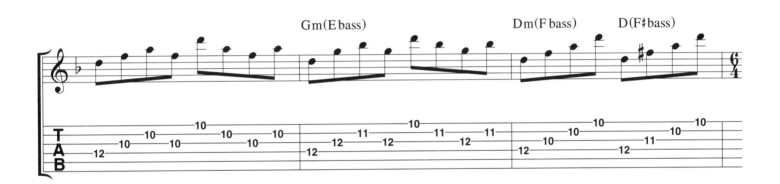

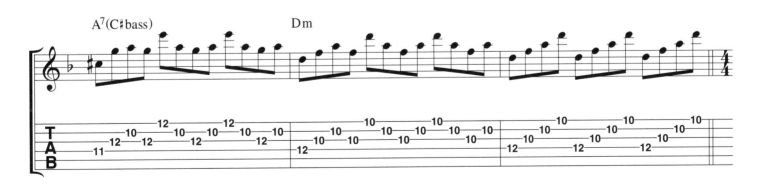

Verse

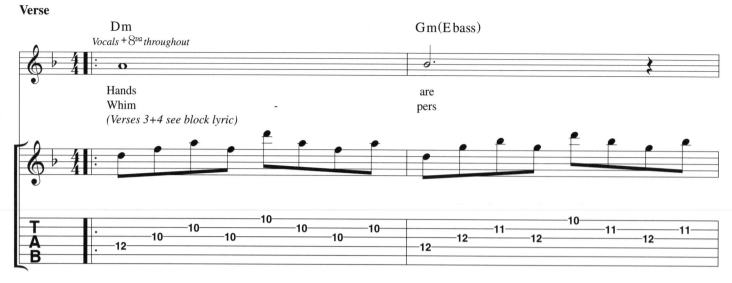

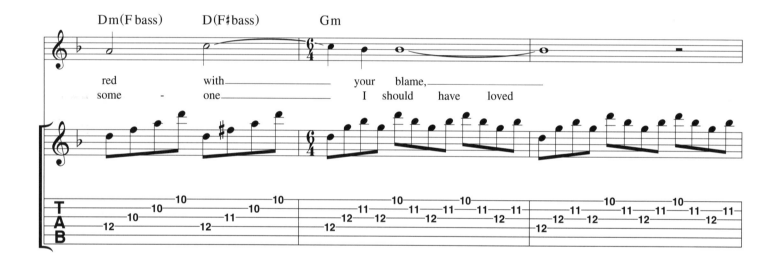

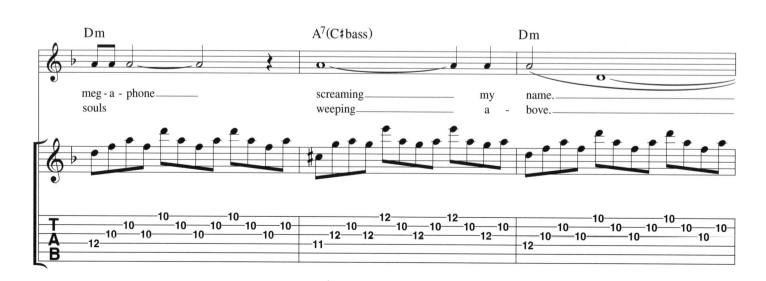

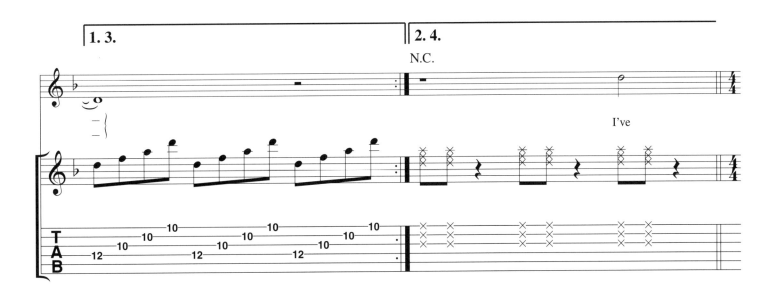

Chorus

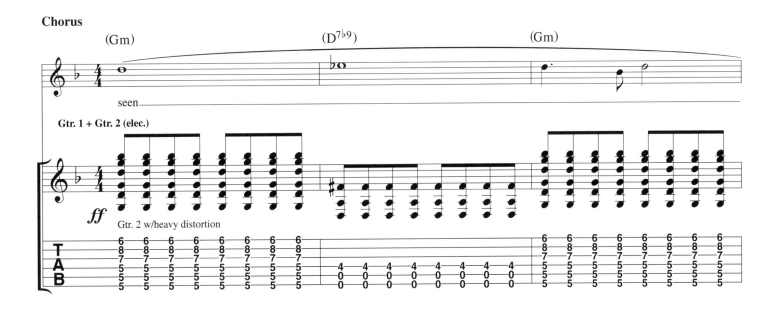

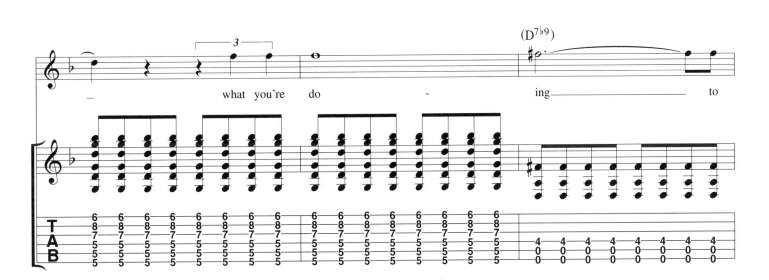

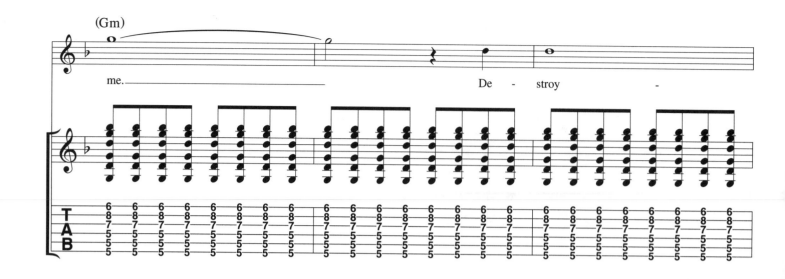

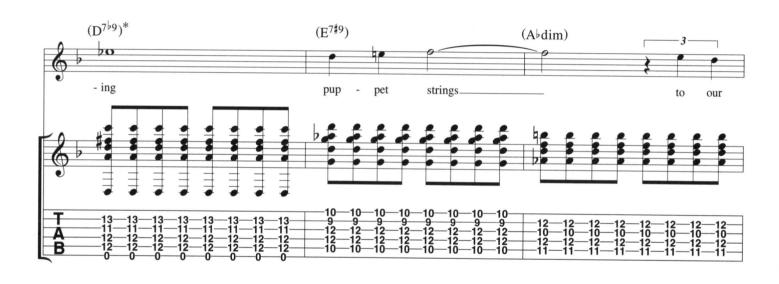

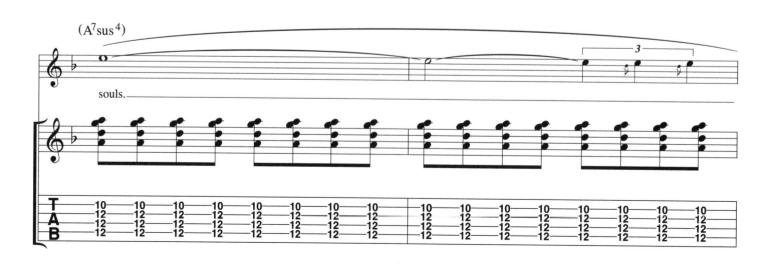

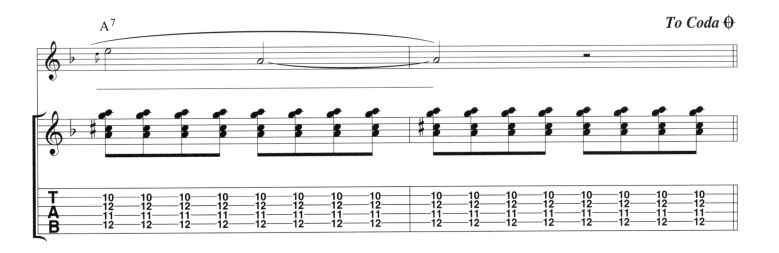

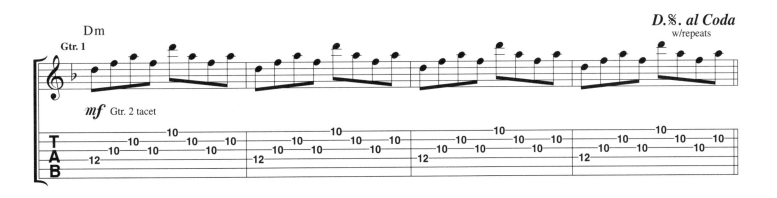

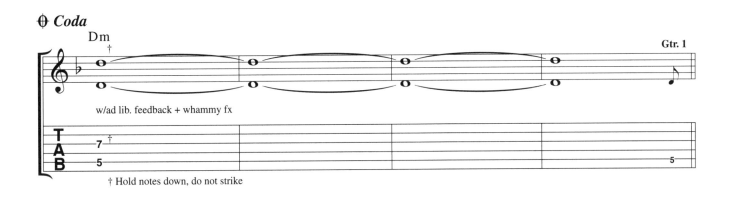

Bridge

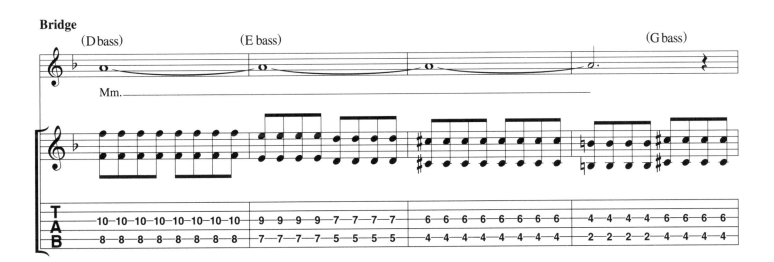

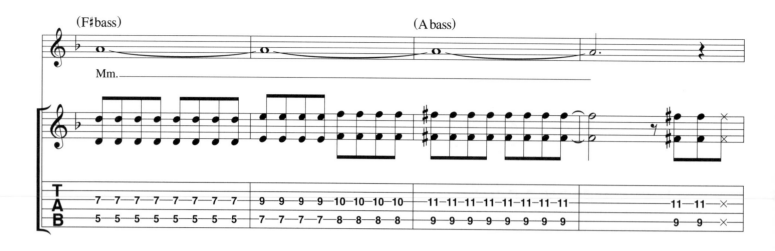

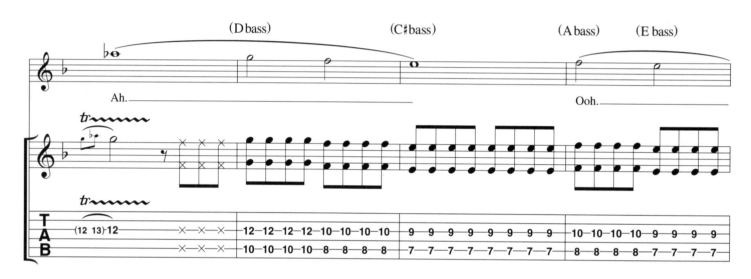

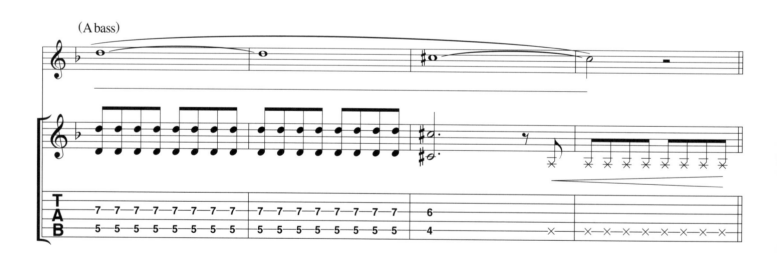

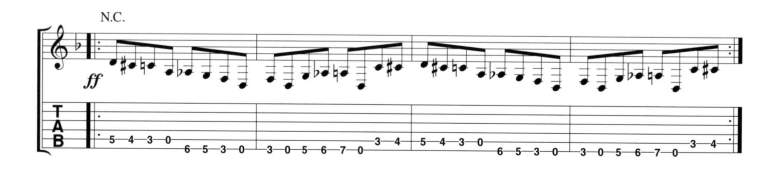

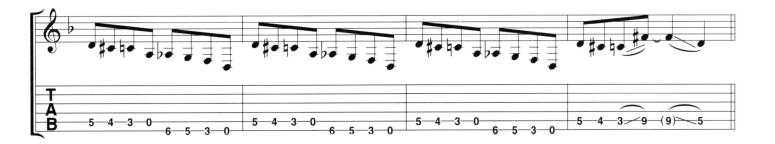

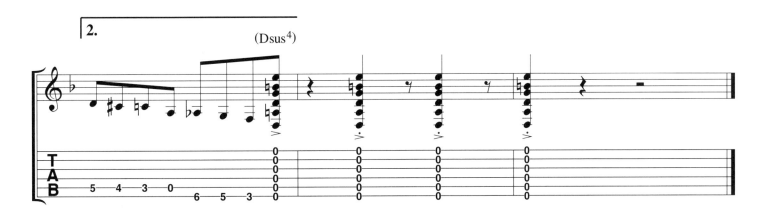

Verse 3:
Microwaves make me insane
A blade cuts into your brain.

Verse 4:
To sounds like a fork on a plate
Blackboard scratched with hate.

Screenager

LYRICS & MUSIC BY MATTHEW BELLAMY

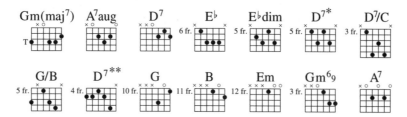

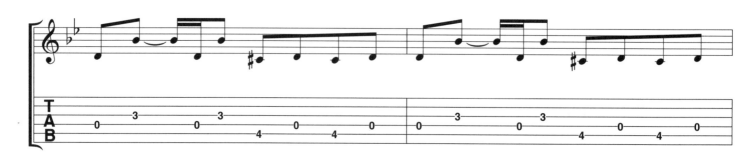

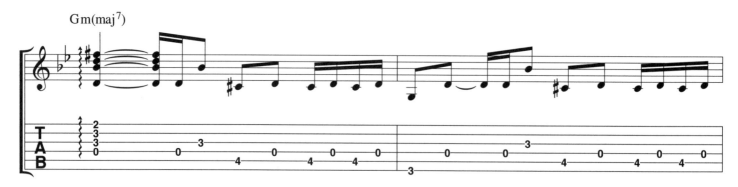

Verse

1. Who's so pho - ney and al - ways sur - round -
2. Hide from the mir - ror the cracks and the mem -

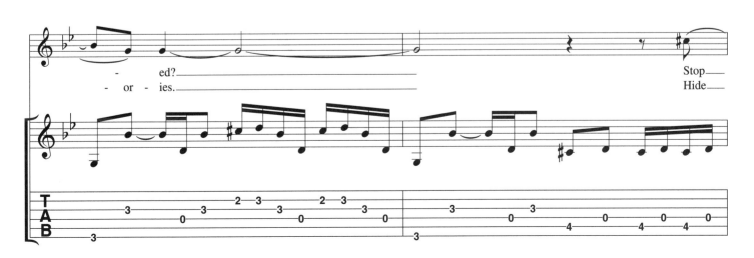

- ed? Stop
- or - ies. Hide

Chorus

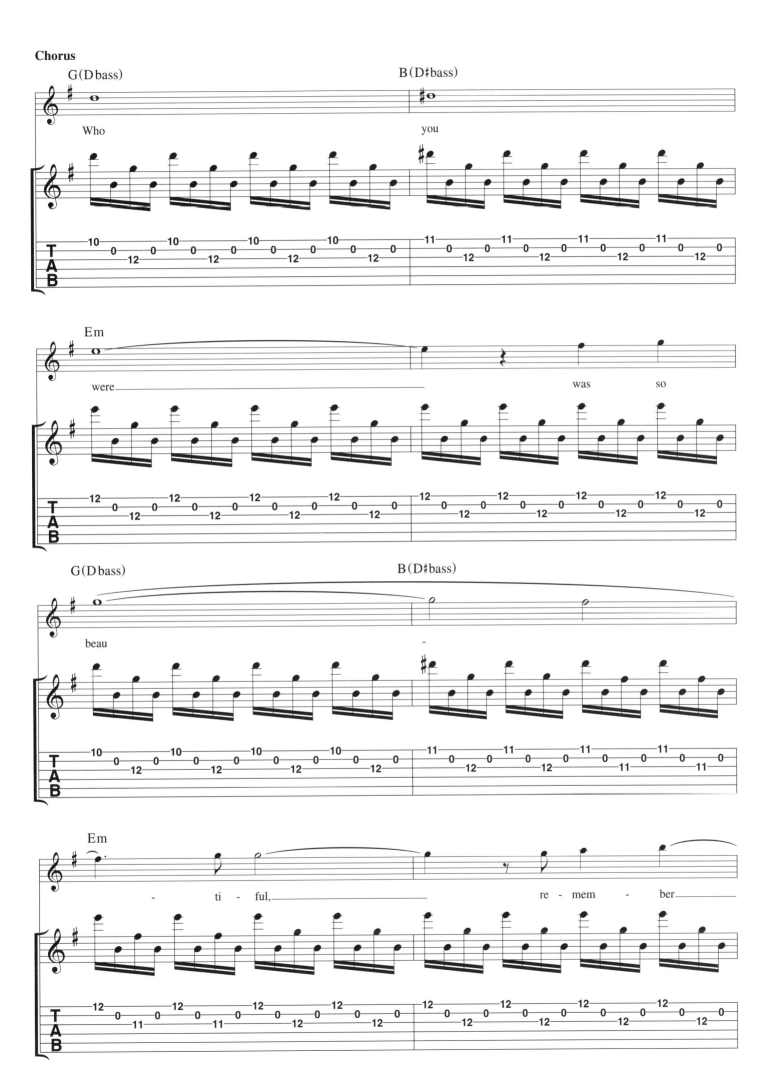

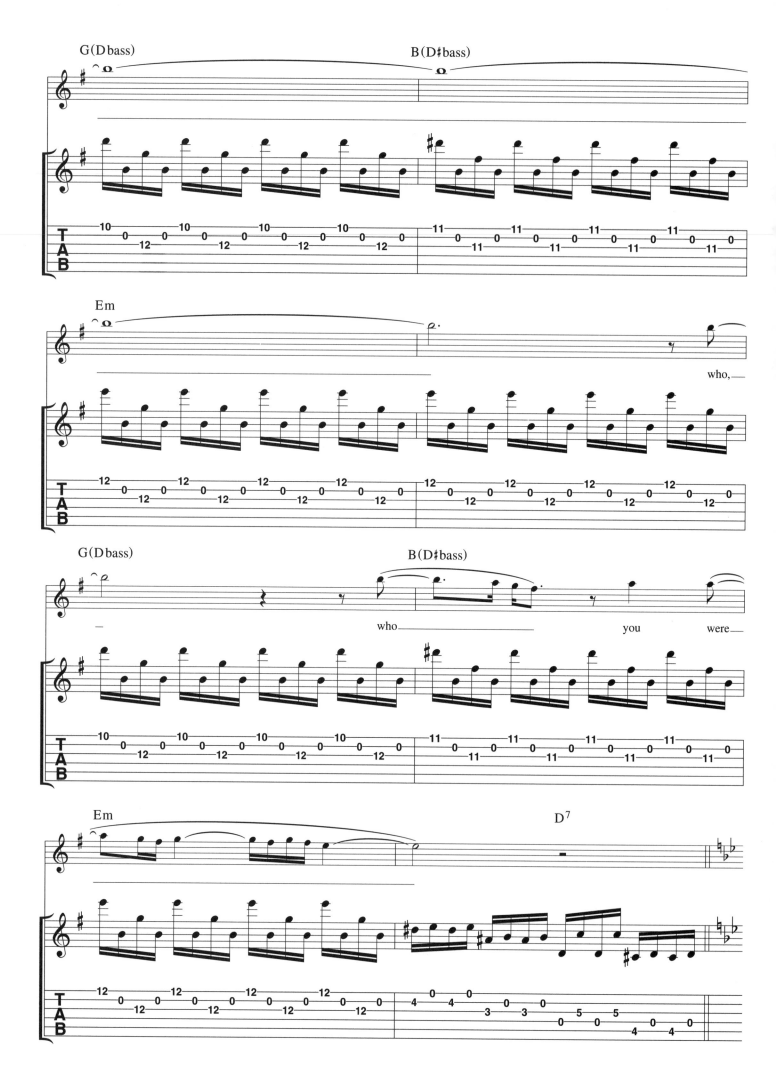

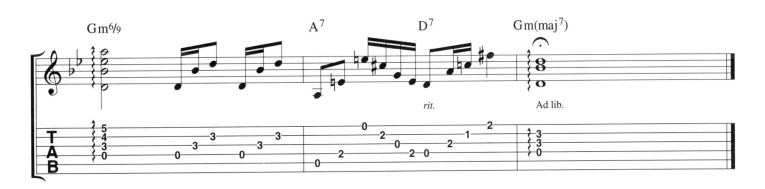

Feeling Good

LYRICS & MUSIC BY LESLIE BRICUSSE & ANTHONY NEWLEY

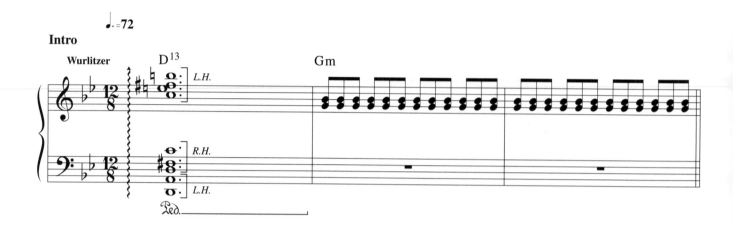

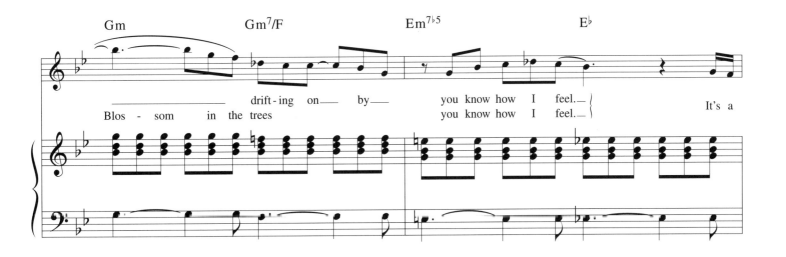

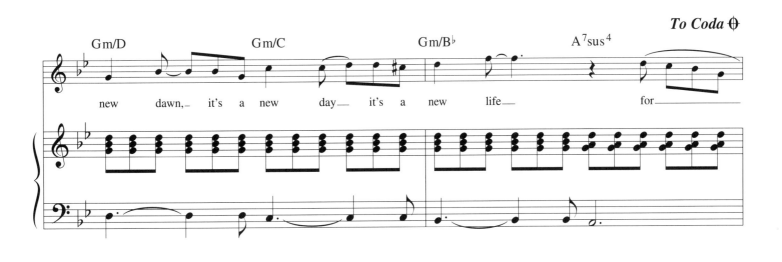

in peace, _____ when day is done ____ and this

old world ___ is a new world, ___ and a bold world _____ for

D.%. al Coda

Gm   Gm/F   Gm/Eb   Gm/D

me.

Piano

Coda

C7   **Bridge**   A

me. ____   feel-ing good. _____   ooh ____

Elec. Piano

f

Verse 3:
Stars when you shine, you know how I feel
Scent of the pine, you know how I feel
Yeah, freedom is mine
And you know how I feel
It's a new dawn, it's a new day, it's a new life for me.

Dark Shines

LYRICS & MUSIC BY MATTHEW BELLAMY

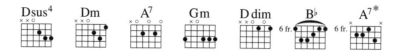

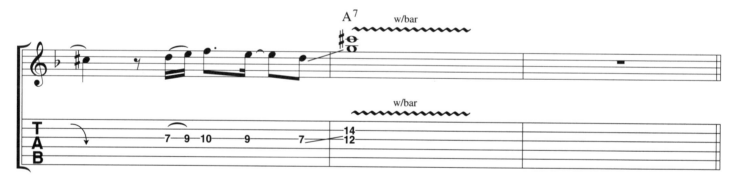

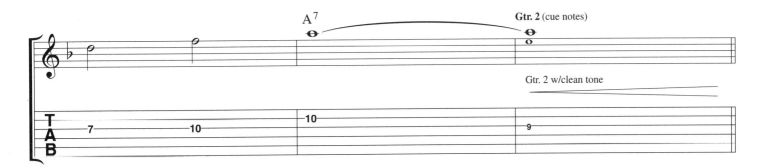

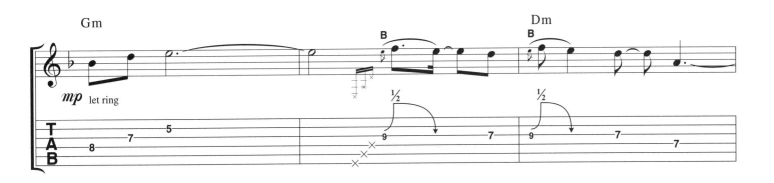

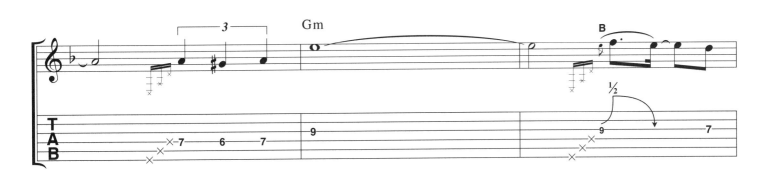

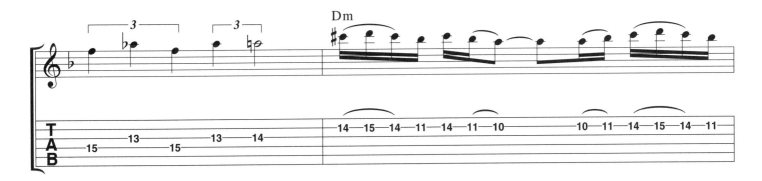

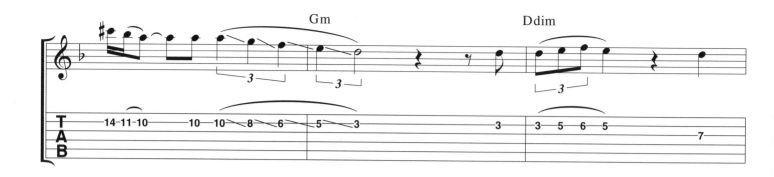

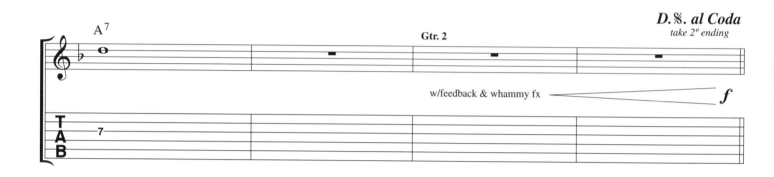

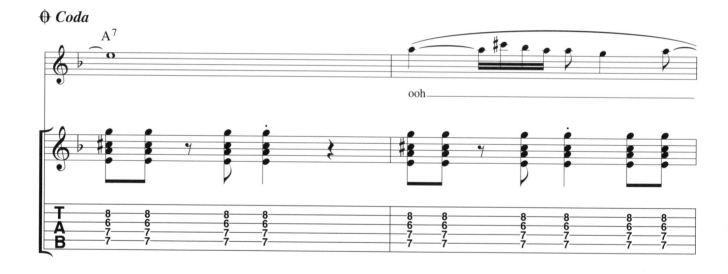

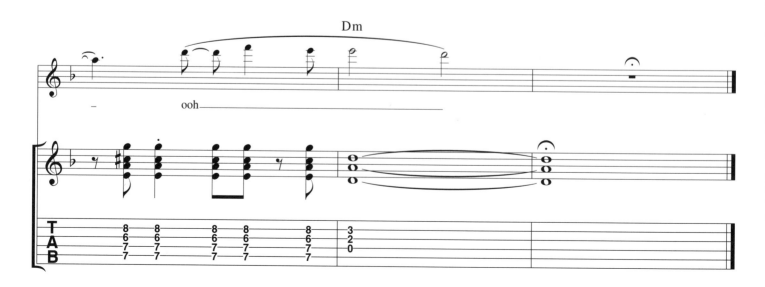

Megalomania

LYRICS & MUSIC BY MATTHEW BELLAMY

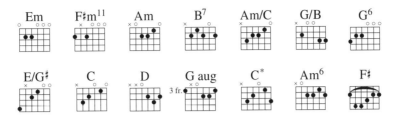

Could some - one tell me please.
long be - fore I dis - turb you in the dark.

The good news is she can't have
And par - a - dise comes at a

ba - bies, and won't ac - cept gifts from me.
price that I am not pre - pared to pay.

What are they for? They'll just

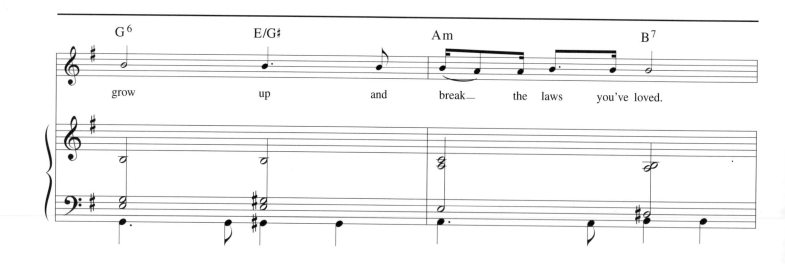

grow up and break— the laws you've loved.

Gtr. tacet

Organ

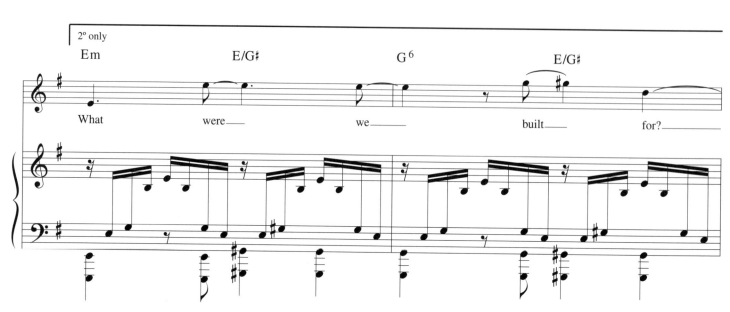

2° only

What were— we— built— for?———

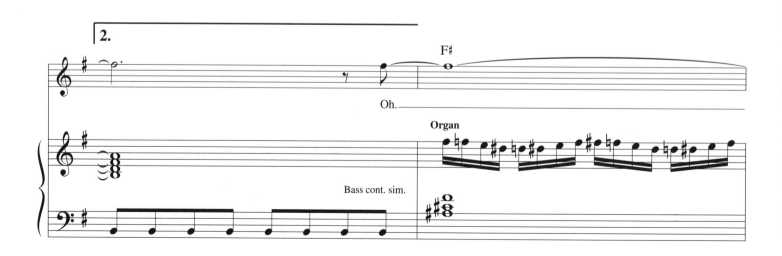

Guitar Tablature Explained

Guitar music can be notated three different ways: on a musical stave, in tablature, and in rhythm slashes

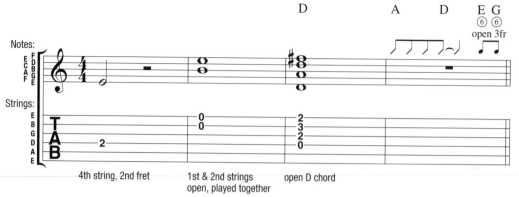

RHYTHM SLASHES are written above the stave. Strum chords in the rhythm indicated. Round noteheads indicate single notes.

THE MUSICAL STAVE shows pitches and rhythms and is divided by lines into bars. Pitches are named after the first seven letters of the alphabet.

TABLATURE graphically represents the guitar fingerboard. Each horizontal line represents a string, and each number represents a fret.

4th string, 2nd fret

1st & 2nd strings open, played together

open D chord

definitions for special guitar notation

SEMI-TONE BEND: Strike the note and bend up a semi-tone (1/2 step).

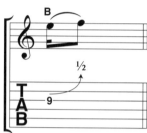

WHOLE-TONE BEND: Strike the note and bend up a whole-tone (whole step).

GRACE NOTE BEND: Strike the note and bend as indicated. Play the first note as quickly as possible.

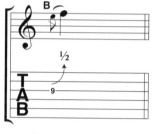

QUARTER-TONE BEND: Strike the note and bend up a 1/4 step.

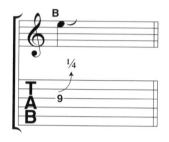

BEND & RELEASE: Strike the note and bend up as indicated, then release back to the original note.

COMPOUND BEND & RELEASE: Strike the note and bend up and down in the rhythm indicated.

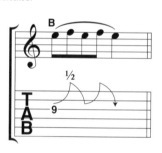

PRE-BEND: Bend the note as indicated, then strike it.

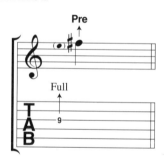

PRE-BEND & RELEASE: Bend the note as indicated. Strike it and release the note back to the original pitch.

UNISON BEND: Strike the two notes simultaneously and bend the lower note up to the pitch of the higher.

BEND & RESTRIKE: Strike the note and bend as indicated then restrike the string where the symbol occurs.

BEND, HOLD AND RELEASE: Same as bend and release but hold the bend for the duration of the tie.

BEND AND TAP: Bend the note as indicated and tap the higher fret while still holding the bend.

VIBRATO: The string is vibrated by rapidly bending and releasing the note with the fretting hand.

HAMMER-ON: Strike the first (lower) note with one finger, then sound the higher note (on the same string) with another finger by fretting it without picking.

PULL-OFF: Place both fingers on the notes to be sounded, Strike the first note and without picking, pull the finger off to sound the second (lower) note.

LEGATO SLIDE (GLISS): Strike the first note and then slide the same fret-hand finger up or down to the second note. The second note is not struck.

NOTE: The speed of any bend is indicated by the music notation and tempo.

SHIFT SLIDE (GLISS & RESTRIKE): Same as legato slide, except the second note is struck.

TRILL: Very rapidly alternate between the notes indicated by continuously hammering on and pulling off.

TAPPING: Hammer ("tap") the fret indicated with the pick-hand index or middle finger and pull off to the note fretted by the fret hand.

PICK SCRAPE: The edge of the pick is rubbed down (or up) the string, producing a scratchy sound.

MUFFLED STRINGS: A percussive sound is produced by laying the fret hand across the string(s) without depressing, and striking them with the pick hand.

NATURAL HARMONIC: Strike the note while the fret-hand lightly touches the string directly over the fret indicated.

PINCH HARMONIC: The note is fretted normally and a harmonic is produced by adding the edge of the thumb or the tip of the index finger of the pick hand to the normal pick attack.

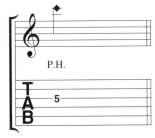

HARP HARMONIC: The note is fretted normally and a harmonic is produced by gently resting the pick hand's index finger directly above the indicated fret (in parentheses) while the pick hand's thumb or pick assists by plucking the appropriate string.

PALM MUTING: The note is partially muted by the pick hand lightly touching the string(s) just before the bridge.

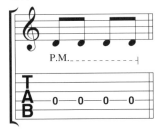

RAKE: Drag the pick across the strings indicated with a single motion.

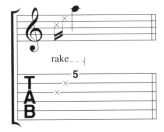

TREMOLO PICKING: The note is picked as rapidly and continuously as possible.

ARPEGGIATE: Play the notes of the chord indicated by quickly rolling them from bottom to top.

SWEEP PICKING: Rhythmic downstroke and/or upstroke motion across the strings.

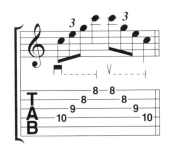

VIBRATO DIVE BAR AND RETURN: The pitch of the note or chord is dropped a specific number of steps (in rhythm) then returned to the original pitch.

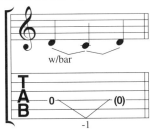

VIBRATO BAR SCOOP: Depress the bar just before striking the note, then quickly release the bar.

VIBRATO BAR DIP: Strike the note and then immediately drop a specific number of steps, then release back to the original pitch.

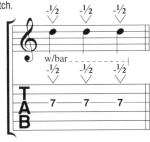

additional musical definitions

 (accent) • Accentuate note (play it louder).

 (accent) • Accentuate note with great intensity.

 (staccato) • Shorten time value of note.

⊓ • Downstroke

∨ • Upstroke

D.%. al Coda

D.C. al Fine

tacet

• Go back to the sign (%), then play until the bar marked *To Coda* ⊕ then skip to the section marked ⊕ *Coda*.

• Go back to the beginning of the song and play until the bar marked *Fine* (end).

• Instrument is silent (drops out).

• Repeat bars between signs.

• When a repeated section has different endings, play the first ending only the first time and the second ending only the second time.

NOTE: Tablature numbers in parentheses mean: 1. The note is sustained, but a new articulation (such as hammer on or slide) begins.
2. A note may be fretted but not necessarily played.

Présentation De La Tablature De Guitare

Il existe trois façons différentes de noter la musique pour guitare : à l'aide d'une portée musicale, de tablatures ou de barres rythmiques.

Les BARRES RYTHMIQUES sont indiquées au-dessus de la portée. Jouez les accords dans le rythme indiqué. Les notes rondes indiquent des notes réciles.

La PORTÉE MUSICALE indique les notes et rythmes et est divisée en mesures. Cette division est représentée par des lignes. Les notes sont : do, ré, mi, fa, sol, la, si.

La PORTÉE EN TABLATURE est une représentation graphique des touches de guitare. Chaque ligne horizontale correspond à une corde et chaque chiffre correspond à une case.

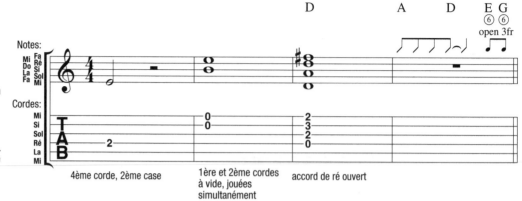

4ème corde, 2ème case   1ère et 2ème cordes à vide, jouées simultanément   accord de ré ouvert

Notation Spéciale De Guitare : Définitions

TIRÉ DEMI-TON : Jouez la note et tirez la corde afin d'élever la note d'un demi-ton (étape à moitié).

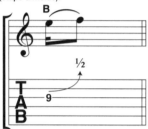

TIRÉ PLEIN : Jouez la note et tirez la corde afin d'élever la note d'un ton entier (étape entière).

TIRÉ D'AGRÉMENT : Jouez la note et tirez la corde comme indiqué. Jouez la première note aussi vite que possible.

TIRÉ QUART DE TON : Jouez la note et tirez la corde afin d'élever la note d'un quart de ton.

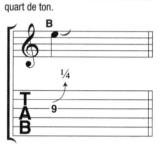

TIRÉ ET LÂCHÉ : Jouez la note et tirez la corde comme indiqué, puis relâchez, afin d'obtenir de nouveau la note de départ.

TIRÉ ET REJOUÉ : Jouez la note et tirez la corde comme indiqué puis rejouez la corde où le symbole apparaît.

PRÉ-TIRÉ : Tirez la corde comme indiqué puis jouez cette note.

PRÉ-TIRÉ ET LÂCHÉ : Tirez la corde comme indiqué. Jouez la note puis relâchez la corde afin d'obtenir le ton de départ.

HAMMER-ON: Jouez la première note (plus basse) avec un doigt puis jouez la note plus haute sur la même corde avec un autre doigt, sur le manche mais sans vous servir du médiator.

PULL-OFF: Positionnez deux doigts sur les notes à jouer. Jouez la première note et sans vous servir du médiator, dégagez un doigt pour obtenir la deuxième note, plus basse.

GLISSANDO : Jouez la première note puis faites glisser le doigt le long du manche pour obtenir la seconde note qui, elle, n'est pas jouée.

GLISSANDO ET REJOUÉ : Identique au glissando à ceci près que la seconde note est jouée.

HARMONIQUES NATURELLES : Jouez la note tandis qu'un doigt effleure la corde sur le manche correspondant à la case indiquée.

PICK SCRAPE (SCRATCH) : On fait glisser le médiator le long de la corde, ce qui produit un son éraillé.

ÉTOUFFÉ DE LA PAUME : La note est partiellement étouffée par la main (celle qui se sert du médiator). Elle effleure la (les) corde(s) juste au-dessus du chevalet.

CORDES ÉTOUFFÉES : Un effet de percussion produit en posant à plat la main sur le manche sans relâcher, puis en jouant les cordes avec le médiator.

NOTE: La vitesse des tirés est indiquée par la notation musicale et le tempo.

Erläuterung zur Tabulaturschreibweise

Es gibt drei Möglichkeiten, Gitarrenmusik zu notieren: im klassichen Notensystem, in Tabulaturform oder als rhythmische Akzente.

RHYTHMISCHE AKZENTE werden über dem Notensystem notiert. Geschlagene Akkorde werden rhythmisch dargestellt. Ausgeschriebene Noten stellen Einzeltöne dar.

Im **NOTENSYSTEM** werden Tonhöhe und rhythmischer Verlauf festgelegt; es ist durch Taktstriche in Takte unterteilt. Die Töne werden nach den ersten acht Buchstaben des Alphabets benannt.
Beachte: "B" in der anglo-amerkanischen Schreibweise entspricht dem deutschen "H"!

DIE TABULATUR ist die optische Darstellung des Gitarrengriffbrettes. Jeder horizontalen Linie ist eine bestimmte Saite zugeordnet, jede Zahl bezeichnet einen Bund.

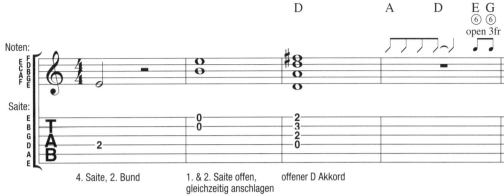

4. Saite, 2. Bund   1. & 2. Saite offen, gleichzeitig anschlagen   offener D Akkord

Erklärungen zur speziellen Gitarennotation

HALBTON-ZIEHER: Spiele die Note und ziehe dann um einen Halbton höher (Halbtonschritt).

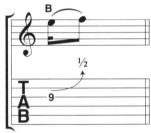

GANZTON-ZIEHER: Spiele die Note und ziehe dann einen Ganzton höher (Ganztonschritt).

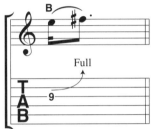

ZIEHER MIT VORSCHLAG: Spiele die Note und ziehe wie notiert. Spiele die erste Note so schnell wie möglich.

VIERTELTON-ZIEHER: Spiele die Note und ziehe dann einen Viertelton höher (Vierteltonschritt).

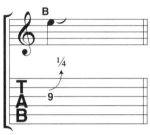

ZIEHEN UND ZURÜCKGLEITEN: Spiele die Note und ziehe wie notiert; lasse den Finger dann in die Ausgangposition zurückgleiten. Dabei wird nur die erste Note angeschlagen.

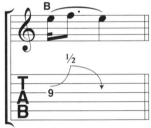

ZIEHEN UND NOCHMALIGES ANSCHLAGEN: Spiele die Note und ziehe wie notiert, schlage die Saite neu an, wenn das Symbol "►" erscheint und lasse den Finger dann zurückgleiten.

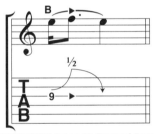

ZIEHER VOR DEM ANSCHLAGEN: Ziehe zuerst die Note wie notiert; schlage die Note dann an.

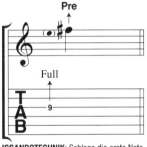

ZIEHER VOR DEM ANSCHLAGEN MIT ZURÜCKGLEITEN: Ziehe die Note wie notiert; schlage die Note dann an und lasse den Finger auf die Ausgangslage zurückgleiten.

AUFSCHLAGTECHNIK: Schlage die erste (tiefere) Note an; die höhere Note (auf der selben Saite) erklingt durch kräftiges Aufschlagen mit einem anderen Finger der Griffhand.

ABZIEHTECHNIK: Setze beide Finger auf die zu spielenden Noten und schlage die erste Note an. Ziehe dann (ohne nochmals anzuschlagen) den oberen Finger der Griffhand seitlich - abwärts ab, um die zweite (tiefere) Note zum klingen zu bringen.

GLISSANDOTECHNIK: Schlage die erste Note an und rutsche dann mit dem selben Finger der Griffhand aufwärts oder abwärts zur zweiten Note. Die zweite Note wird nicht angeschlagen.

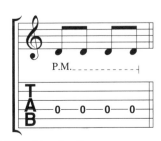

GLISSANDOTECHNIK MIT NACHFOLGENDEM ANSCHLAG: Gleiche Technik wie das gebundene Glissando, jedoch wird die zweite Note angeschlagen.

NATÜRLICHES FLAGEOLETT: Berühre die Saite über den angegebenen Bund leicht mit einem Finger der Griffhand. Schlage die Saite an und lasse sie frei schwingen.

PICK SCRAPE: Fahre mit dem Plektrum nach unten über die Saiten - klappt am besten bei umsponnenen Saiten.

DÄMPFEN MIT DER SCHLAGHAND: Lege die Schlaghand oberhalb der Brücke leicht auf die Saite(n).

DÄMPFEN MIT DER GRIFFHAND: Du erreichst einen percussiven Sound, indem du die Griffhand leicht über die Saiten legst (ohne diese herunterzudrücken) und dann mit der Schlaghand anschlägst.

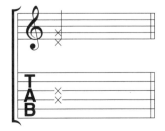

AMMERKUNG: Das Tempo der Zieher und Glissandos ist abhängig von der rhythmischen Notation und dem Grundtempo.